ANNE BRUNSWIC

I0441382

WELCOME
TO PALESTINE

CHRONICLES OF A SEASON
IN RAMALLAH

Translated by Kenneth Casler

Also by Anne Brunswic

A contre-oubli, La Fontaine-aux-Loups/Delphine Montalant, 2000.
Qu'est-ce que tu fais là ?, La Fontaine-aux-Loups/Delphine Montalant, 2001.
Bienvenue en Palestine, chroniques d'une saison à Ramallah, Actes Sud, 2004. RFI-Témoin du monde award 2004.
Sibérie, un voyage au pays des femmes, Actes Sud 2006.
Les eaux glacées du Belomorkanal, Actes Sud 2009.

www.annebrunswic.fr

© Cover : Robert Radford, High Tension , after Anne Brunswic's picture of the wall in Qalandiya'h, 2006.

© Actes Sud 2004
© Babel 2006 (New expanded edition)
© Translation 2008

To my Uncle Etienne

Our inheritance was left to us by no document.

RENÉ CHAR

And even if the Jews were to win the war, its end would find the unique possibilities and the unique achievements of Zionism in Palestine destroyed. The land that would come into being would be something quite other than the dream of world Jewry, Zionist and non-Zionist. The "victorious" Jews would live surrounded by an entirely hostile Arab population, secluded inside ever-threatened borders, absorbed with physical self-defense to a degree that would submerge all other interests and activities. The growth of a Jewish culture would cease to be the concern of the whole people ; social experiments would have to be discarded as impractical luxuries ; political thought would center around military strategy ; economic development would be determined exclusively by the needs of war.

HANNAH ARENDT
" To Save the Jewish Homeland ",
in *Commentary*, May 1948, p. 403.

4

Friday, October 3, 2003, Ramallah

Here Friday is like Saturday over there, on the neighbour's side, not much traffic in the streets, not a car horn all morning ; a tiny crowd of worshippers at eleven o'clock prayers ; then a small political rally. Otherwise a rather quiet day.

I have been in Ramallah for five days, since last Sunday. I live in a spacious well-furnished flat, a hundred metres from Al-Manara Square ; no problem finding a taxi regardless of destination. I already have a fixed-line phone, a mobile phone and an Internet connection. Many thanks to my Israeli film friends and their contacts. It's so easy to make friends here – in the streets, in cafés, in taxis, on campus, with neighbours and shopkeepers. Christian or Muslim, English-speaker or French-speaker, Palestinians are always happy to welcome a guest.

Everyday life here is not what you would expect from a country at war. To be sure, Arafat's compound, the Muqataa, only a kilometre away, can be targeted by the Israeli army at any time. Built under

British occupation, the compound's two large buildings housed the offices of the security forces until the autumn of 2002. Today it is little more than a pile of ruins : floors collapsed on top of each other, clumps of rubble stuck to metal struts, a layer cake of iron and concrete. Only the building occupied by Arafat – Abu Amar as he is known here – still stands, in a wind-swept courtyard.

Israeli soldiers, I'm told, make frequent forays into the city in search of a suspect or just to intimidate. They are young (most are under twenty) and frightened ; they don't understand the reality of the situation. This makes them even more dangerous. They understand very little Arabic and among themselves most speak Russian. Armed to the teeth in a conquered land, heads full of video games, these teen-aged newcomers to Israeli society fancy they are somebody, or something important.

To tell the truth the last Israeli soldier I saw was last Sunday, when I passed through the Kalandia checkpoint (I wasn't even asked to show my ID). Not a single Palestinian policeman, except the one directing traffic feebly at a roundabout and the three characters huddled near a wooden shed bearing a portrait of Arafat and serving as a guard post at the entrance of the presidential building. None of them is wearing a uniform, to avoid becoming a target.

The Jewish settlers on the surrounding hilltops are invisible. They no longer move about in Ramallah and haven't fired one shot from their eagle's nests for some time.

Ramallah, I'm told, is the Champs-Elysées of Palestine : a rich city with a large Christian and Muslim bourgeoisie. Luxury stores and villas with gardens –

holiday homes built in the 1930s by Arab families from the Emirates – are plentiful. It seems the Gulf Arabs appreciated the city's climate, particularly its cool summer evenings. Many of Ramallah's residents have been to university in Palestine, Europe and the United States ; many have relatives in America. Three thousand civil servants work for the Palestinian administration. Some two hundred foreigners are employed by international organisations, NGOs and cultural services. Every evening they fill the city centre's five cafés, where beer and wine are served until midnight.

The architecture, landscape, the atmosphere of the busy shopping streets remind me of what I knew in Jerusalem in the mid 1960s, when I first went to visit my grandmother. The landscape of endless desert hills stretches northwest from my balcony as far as I can see. The same white stone as in Jerusalem covers the facades of even the most recent buildings. The same pleasant scents of jasmine and fig, lemon tree and bougainvillea float in the garden below. The same lively confusion reigns near the taxi rank at the upper end of the street, where boys serve coffee to waiting drivers. The same carpets are laid in my flat on the same sand-coloured stippled tiles. The same marble around the basin ; the same spacious rooms.

In the district of Ramallah resistance to the occupation is dull, except in the refugee camps. In the north near the Jalazone refugee camp and in the south around the Kalandia camp, the army patrols are regularly hit by young people throwing stones.

If Ramallah is Palestine's Champs-Elysées, Gaza is its working class suburb ; Jenin and Nablus lie somewhere in between. Social class is clearly visible here, and the different classes, people say, mix no better than oil and water.

The headscarf expresses subtle social distinctions that, for the moment anyway, still escape me. Monday evening, for example, at an event in honour of Edward Said – the audience made up primarily of the local elite – not one woman in the room wears a headscarf; outside, in the street, there is not one without. Last Friday, at a sumptuous lunch with the Huzris, my neighbours in the flat on the same floor, the sixty-year-old mother wore her traditional garments and headscarf; in contrast, her daughters and daughters-in-law did not cover their heads. One of the daughters is a professor of science at the local technical college (financed by the United Nations); the other is finishing her degree in Journalism at Bir Zeit University; her daughter-in-law works for a bank.

Majid, my neighbour's eldest son, speaks fluent French (he studied law in France). Thirty-five years old, tall and well-built, he looks like many Palestinian men. He is in charge of diplomatic relations with France, travels to Paris frequently and heads the official welcome committee for visiting delegations in Ramallah. " The students who threw stones at Prime Minister Jospin[1] were properly punished and expelled from university, for a few months anyway ", he explains. " We have only one friend in Europe, France. It's scandalous to treat a friend like that. Our President immediately presented an apology. " Majid is determined to confront the extremists and to do so

---

[1] The Prime Minister of France, Lionel Jospin, visited Bir Zeit University in February, 2000. He was stoned after labelling Hizbollah a terrorist organisation (trans. note).

as soon as possible. It is a matter of the Palestinian Authority's credibility. He believes in the Authority and in the peaceful coexistence of two separate states.

But Selim Quatab, an activist and leader of a non-violent organisation, does not share Majid's political realism. Fragment of a conversation : " Selim, you have a university degree ; you earn enough money to live outside the refugee camp. Why do you stay there ?

– It's true, I have a flat in Ramallah city, but I return to the camp every evening. My mother lives there ; so do most of my friends. We all come from the same village, near Lod airport. If I left the camp, I would be throwing away a life-long dream. I want to return to my grandfather's village and raise my children there. I'm thirty-three years old and a bachelor. I don't want to raise my children here, in a refugee camp.

– You talk about your dream. If the two-state solution becomes reality, you'll have to give it up. You won't be able to settle within the pre-1967 borders.

– Not necessarily. All I have to do is marry a Jewish girl from the other side and have some children ! "

As a child Selim wanted to be an airline pilot. Instead he studied English, History and Political Science. But his head remains in the clouds and he dreams of a return to his promised land.

What really makes for daily suffering here is humiliation. From the heights above the city, Israeli settlers hold the sixty thousand inhabitants of Ramallah in the crosshairs of their weapons. To the north and south the Israeli army occupies impressive checkpoints, which marksmen protect on tense days.

The military authorities deliver the necessary permits for travel in the West Bank. Every day countless hours are wasted passing through these roadblocks, draining everyone's energy, restricting horizons. Many have not left the city for three years. Not so long ago the trip to Amman took only forty-five minutes ; now it's two days. Going to Jenin took an hour and a half ; there's no telling how long today.

Everyone has his checkpoint story. The latest ? Rami, a civil engineer, went to Jenin with three co-workers the day before yesterday. Since the town is under curfew most of the time, he calls his colleagues in Jenin at four in the morning to get an up-date on the situation. Last Wednesday the curfew was lifted and he was given the green light to travel. He and his team set out by car at seven a.m.. Luckily everyone had a US Aid stamp on his travel permit so the trip took " only " three hours. They finished work as quickly as possible to make it back to Ramallah before their permits expired and reached the last checkpoint at six p.m. The Israeli soldier on guard looked at his watch : " Seven o'clock. Your permits have expired. Your car is impounded. Come with me. – But, it's only six in Palestine ", they protested, " Israel is an hour ahead of us. – Six ? Nonsense ! Give me your watches ! " The soldier confiscated keys, IDs and watches and went to the guard station. Fifteen minutes later a Palestinian worker arrived from Jerusalem. " What time is it ? " the soldier asked. " Seven fifteen ", the worker replies, in Hebrew, " but in Palestine it's six fifteen ; last Saturday we changed over to winter time ; you change next Sunday. " These explanations in Hebrew succeed in convincing the Israeli soldier.

10

Rami adds something to the story. On the way to Jenin the travellers took a back road to avoid certain checkpoints. Somebody says, " Hey, my mother lives close by and I haven't seen her in months. Can we make a short stop so I can say hello ? " At eight in the morning the young man stands outside his mother's building and bangs on the front door. Since the former residents – her children and neighbours – evacuated the building, no one but she lives there any more. With all the noise downstairs the poor lady is so frightened, it's fully ten minutes before she realizes her own son is downstairs at the front door.

Those Palestinians who can avoid contact with Israelis soldiers. They shut themselves in and enjoy the domestic delights of the telephone and Internet. But sometimes soldiers barge right into the living room itself. Last Wednesday, Sally and Shami had a surprise visit in the middle of the night. Sally, a French-speaking Tunisian, described the scene to me.

" The night before last, around eleven-thirty, the soldiers banged at our door. We usually get to bed late, but the day before yesterday my husband and I were really tired ; for once we were in bed early. My husband doesn't wear pyjamas, so when we heard the knocks he jumped up, pulled on some trousers and opened the door. 'Identity check. Everyone out of the building.' There are three flats in our building, and there were six soldiers. They took my husband and our neighbour outside, then started banging on the door of the flat above. As there was no answer, they started to knock it down. My husband shouted : " Wait, the flat's empty. The owners live in the USA. I'll get the key. – Why do you have the key ? " the soldiers ask, suspiciously. – " So you don't break down the door on these raids ! "

Afterwards, the soldiers held all the men in the empty flat, which was covered in dust, for most of the night.

It was a routine operation. The army checks every flat in the neighbourhood and makes a record, listing the names of residents, making a note of fixed-line and mobile phone numbers. Then the information is used to monitor movements of everybody they know.

" The worst is, when the soldiers were done and ready to leave, the officer extended his hand and Shami shook it without thinking. He's so good he can't refuse a handshake. Can you believe it, they try to be polite at the same time ! "

Sally has another story to tell about the " delicacy " of Israeli soldiers. It concerns her friend Jenny.

" Because Jenny lives next to the Muqataa, Israeli soldiers invaded her place at least six times in 2002. Each time they ransacked it completely. Jenny's old mother was still alive then. The last time the Israelis barged in, the old lady had a malaise. The leader said : 'I'm a medical doctor. I'll give her an injection.' Jenny threw a fit : " Don't you dare touch my mother ! I forbid you to touch a single hair on her head ! "

To conclude this first chronicle, a list of memorable moments.

The most pleasant moment : a taxi driver, setting me down in front of the Sudra checkpoint, refuses my two shekels ; Abeer, a science student, insists on paying the two shekels for my return taxi ride home ; the owner of the Tour Eiffel pastry shop refuses to let me pay for his cakes ; at the Internet café Naslim insists on fixing my computer free of charge ; the baker gives me bread for free...It is impossible to list all the small kindnesses I receive every day.

The most exhausting moment : I am in Zyriab café around midnight, the sorry witness to a heated argument between a German geologist and a British filmmaker. Peter, the filmmaker, came to Palestine to shoot a documentary about water scarcity ; he wants to prove that the Israeli settlers are responsible for the growing desertification of the lower Jordan valley. Wilhelm, the German geologist, tries to explain that soil salinization did not appear for the first time in 1948. He peppers his remarks with the names of Liebknecht, Kautsky and a few others. My eyes sting with fatigue ; instincts tell me I am in the wrong place at the wrong time.

The most embarrassing moment : " We are Orthodox Christians and the others don't like us here. Are you Christian ? " my landlady asks. – No, Jewish. – Don't tell anyone. Say you're Christian or only you're French. " I insist, " But Tom and Ada, the previous occupants, were Jews and they never had any problems here ! " – " You never know ", she concludes with finality. Needless to say, all the Palestinian militants I have spoken with in the meantime strongly advise me to answer frankly to frank questions. And, on the contrary, they find me " courageous " and appreciate what I am doing here.

The most official moment : meeting the well-known Israeli journalist, Amira Hass. She bundles me into her old Renault car with TV painted in big letters all over. We drive to a ceremony in honour of Edward Said, which is followed by a candle-light march through the high street of Ramallah. She knows everyone : the handful of journalists, the officials of the Palestinian Authority and the local worthies. I find the speeches in Arabic too difficult to follow. The pretty young woman sitting next to me offers to translate into English. Reem is a final year student in Journalism and Media at Bir Zeit University. She says she would like to see me again and is keen to help in any way she can.

The moment to put on film : the crossing at the Sudra checkpoint on the road to Bir Zeit University. In the bend of a road, winding up through lovely hills towards the university, two huge slabs of concrete block the middle of the road. Eight hundred metres of no man's land separate the two roadblocks ; hundreds of pedestrians move in both directions ; invalids are pushed through in wheelchairs ; goods move across in horse carts ; some carry a few passengers. At each roadblock, two clusters of fifty or more taxis are locked in an inextricable yellow jam. Most students and professors use this road twice a day. " Once it took barely eight to ten minutes to reach the campus from downtown Ramallah by car. Now it's at least an hour. Yesterday, with the usual Thursday evening traffic at the checkpoint, it took over two hours to get home ", Malika, my downstairs neighbour, says. " It's not all bad though. Before, we never had time to chat. Now there's plenty ! " Another student agrees that the forced march offers rewards : " Now at least everyone is on equal footing and we can talk with our professors ! "

The moment to be photographed : a game of cards at an outdoor café around the corner from Clock Square (the clock has disappeared !). The jolly expressions of the bald, potbellied players, the play of lights and shadows on the café terrace, the round table with demitasse cups of coffee and cards strewn across the top, the sleepy activity of an afternoon in Palestine.

The moment of black humour : Mamdhour Nowfal, straight out of an Egyptian B movie, is a large-framed comic character, small grey moustache and smiling half-creased eyes, a former PLO military advisor and Arafat confidant. He tells me this story. A short distance after a checkpoint the driver of a collective taxi hails a passenger for the last seat in his minibus bound for Ramallah. " Last seat to paradise ! – Will you really drop me off in paradise ? – Actually we're going to hell. But paradise is right next door ! "

4 – 10 October

News of the attack in Haifa reaches me in the afternoon : someone from the French cultural centre calls to cancel a dinner engagement for this evening in honour of French-speaking guests in Ramallah. A serious Israeli reprisal is expected. My neighbours rush to the shops for supplies and because their refrigerator is already stuffed full, they ask if they can store some food in mine. They learned their lesson from last year's raids.

How can you predict that something is going to happen in Ramallah ? The answer : spot the " vultures ". This is the name for reporters who stake out positions around the Muqataa compound (there are several on Jenny's roof). Radio Street, the main artery leading to the compound, is completely empty. Just in case, an ambulance is stationed in Al-Manara Square. Fifty or so onlookers gather to watch, in case something happens. Nothing does, strictly nothing. At dusk we hear that Uri Avnery has cut short his Yom Kippur celebrations and is on his way here to protect the president of the Palestinian Authority with two

Israeli and twenty international volunteers. In Israel authorized voices are taking turns calling for an end to Arafat " once and for all, one way or another ".

Sunday. It is quiet outside, but dread fills the air. Last night Israeli tanks were heard on patrol in the town centre. My landlady, Mrs. Huda, has been to mass already (at the Orthodox Church) and has prepared the family lunch. I'm invited. Seated around the table are her husband, her three nieces, Reem, Wardah, May Soun, and her nephew-by-marriage, Nicholas. May Soun and Nicholas are both dancers ; they met at the local arts centre. The handsome young Australian had to show true obstinacy to win the hand of the local girl. Palestinians – both Christians and Muslims – do not willingly give up a daughter to a " foreigner ". Nor does the Orthodox Church. Nicholas got off lightly : he escaped with baptism and two months of catechism. " Any more and I was headed to Cyprus for the wedding. " Today Nicholas is about as Palestinian as he will ever be ; he and May Soun lead artistic workshops for children in the refugee camps and villages near Nablus. " I want the kids to be in touch with their bodies, but not through violence or anger. "

The same evening, an Italian choir from Piedmont gives a concert at the Lutheran church. It is pleasant, but the atmosphere hanging over the tiny audience of bourgeois Christians is churchy. Only two women wear headscarves : two ancient Catholic nuns.

After the concert Sally and Shami planned to stroll over to the Muqataa " to greet some friends ". " Can we take you home or do you want to come along ? " I certainly have no desire to become a human shield...but how can I say no to such an invitation ? A couple of minutes later, on a balmy evening lit by a waxing three-quarters moon, our tiny group pass through the back gate of the Muqataa. Sunday evening, 9 p.m. October 5.

The players : Ilan Halevi, a devilish man oozing intelligence, bearded, stubby legs, who speaks perfect French and constantly plays with a string of worry beads, like a Greek, battling an urge to smoke ; Jenny Labna, also a French-speaker, elegant, approximately the same age as Ilan, who lives next door to the Muqataa, so we pick her up on the way there. The others are Shami Elias, a senior cadre in a Palestinian ministry, his wife Sally and me in the role of " last-minute guest ". Shami, very tall with a high forehead and a soft voice, and Sally, small and talkative.

The setting is inspired, perfect for a stage director. The outer perimeter is a wall of naked concrete topped by barbed wire a metre high. It looks like a construction site or a municipal dump. Three guards, armed but out of uniform, allow our group through the gate ; they greet Ilan Halevi with a familiar smile, as if he were a resident here. Sally whispers that Ilan is the European affairs advisor to the Ministry of International Cooperation and the Fatah representative to the Socialist International. Nobody checks our IDs. It is hard to believe that the Muqataa is on high alert this evening.

We enter a roughly asphalted esplanade, which once served as the presidential helipad, when Arafat still enjoyed some freedom of movement ; four official cars are parked there now. High piles of rubble – earth, rocks, concrete, girders, stones, twisted metal – frame three sides of the enclosure. Between two mounds of rubble, a poorly lit hut of green boards ; it houses the Presidential Guard ; no more than twenty security personnel.

On the right a heap of burned-out cars fly the Palestinian flag and blocks the entrance to the official courtyard. The three buildings, one on each side – the sole survivors of the last Israeli raid – form an almost perfect quadrilateral, roughly forty metres wide. The oldest, made of ochre coloured stone, was a prison under the British occupation ; it has a blind facade. The other two, more recent, made of whiter stone, have the same proportions as the former prison – massive windowless cubes.

A sheet with a painted portrait of Arafat hangs from one of the facades. On another wall hand-written bills are plastered like in a high school courtyard on a protest day. A flickering street lamp lights the scene sporadically. A dozen plastic chairs form a circle near the wall.

Uri Avnery sits there, recognisable by his thick white hair, elegant white beard and thin silhouette of an old " young pioneer " wearing a black tee shirt and jeans. The respected president of Gush Shalom (the Peace Bloc) celebrated his eightieth birthday last month. His wife Rachel, talking on her mobile phone with friends in Israel, gives him the latest news. " Ariel Sharon has just declared that Arafat's fate is sealed ; he is condemned. " Rachel and Uri – it is said they never do anything without the other – look alike : she is as tanned and slender as he, just as youthful with her large cap pulled down over her thick hair, a thin voice. To protect him from the approaching evening chill she lovingly drapes a plaid shirt over her man's shoulders. He continues to answer the questions of the journalist seated opposite him as he slips it on.

" Can Yasser Arafat put a stop to the terrorist attacks ". " Arafat won't start a civil war. The Palestinian movement went through that in 1948 ; it won't happen again. Even if Arafat did arrest thirty leaders of the extremist groups, they would be replaced immediately. Believe me, when a terrorist movement enjoys popular support, you can put as many leaders in prison as you like, nothing changes. The British locked up the leaders of the Stern group ; the attacks still continued. I know ; I was fifteen when I first joined a terrorist group. I was in a state of shock because, for the first time, the British had executed a Jewish leader. And when an entire population is in such a state, nothing can stop terrorism. Only when people see concrete steps in favour of peace will violence taper off. "

The journalist scribbles notes in a spiral notebook. Avnery speaks clearly, simply, matter-of-factly. He is a professional politician. At this moment his life is on the line. If Israeli soldiers storm the compound, as in the past, he can be killed. His death would be called an " unfortunate accident ". He makes no mention of this now. No reason ; he did so yesterday at an improvised press conference. He and a few volunteers reacted immediately " to protect Arafat, to prevent an assassination that would drown the region in a bloodbath. "

This is not the first time Uri and Rachel Avnery have set up camp in the Muqataa compound : last month they were here when the Israeli Knesset voted the elimination of Arafat, regardless of how, including assassination.

In a brightly lit room, at right angles to the courtyard, the " internationals " are settled in. Thirty mattresses line the floor. A few militants are trying to nap ; some are chatting ; others are talking with the soldiers on guard. There are a few Americans, retired teachers pushing seventy, and an Englishman, not much younger, the author of an essay on Marxism and humanism. Surprise, there is also a Japanese singer, wearing Afro dreadlocks and listening to music through earphones. Three young Italian girls practice their juggling skills to the delight of the soldiers. Two young Israeli anarchists, twenty-year-olds, stretch out on white plastic chairs next to a table covered with sandwiches and orangeade. In total, the twenty people hanging around at this late hour are incapable of filling the high-ceilinged, bare-walled room. The glaring neon lights work a chilling effect.

A few Palestinians drop by as old friends, like Sally and Shami, to greet the volunteers, whose only motivation for taking such personal risks is their moral commitment. The lightly armed guards without uniforms continue to ogle the female jugglers.

In the courtyard Uri Avnery is joined by Ilan Halevi, who earlier on arrival disappeared into the floors of the building on the left to greet Abu Amar. The conversation now turns to Shimon Peres, the eternal loser, the chronic fake. " He never won an election in his life, a true accomplishment for a professional politician ", Avnery sneers. He delights in giving the dates and facts of Peres's political career. " He wasted every opportunity ; he ordered the assassination of the Hamas chief in Gaza to win votes that finally went to Netanyahou. – Peres lied to everybody but Sharon ", Ilan Halevi chimes in. The complicity between Avnery and Halevi, two wily politicians, bearded, shrewd, smiling, is palpable.

22

Seated side by side in the courtyard, the two confederates trade stories with grand gestures ; they have been telling them for ages ; still the two journalists attentively take notes and a few friends sit listening in a circle of plastic chairs. The lights in the courtyard flicker on and off and sometimes the two men disappear from sight, only their deep-throated laughs echoing in the dark.

It's nearly eleven p.m., time to rest for those who will spend the night and probably the next few days in the Muqataa.

Monday. The circumstances of the Haifa attack are somewhat clearer. Everybody I meet condemns the attack, even before I can ask the question. They do not like civilians to die regardless of whether they are Israeli or Palestinian ; " It's against the teaching of every religion ", confirm both Mrs. Huda, my Christian landlady, and Darwich, the Muslim filmmaker. They know the price will be disproportionately high in reprisals – absurdly high. Not to mention the political price ; every attack gives the Israeli government a pretext to intensify colonisation and postpone the implementation of the roadmap. Yet everyone spares a thought for the young female suicide bomber, a twenty-seven-year-old lawyer, whose brother and husband were killed before her eyes (rumour has it they were tortured). Hamas, I'm told, condemned the attack because it disapproves of female suicide bombers. Only a few, like the economist Hael al-Fahoum (the former second-in-command of the PLO in Paris), put the blame firmly on Sharon for creating the circumstances ; but also on the fundamentalists for objectively lending a hand ; and on the Palestinian demagogues for paying mere lip service to the disavowal. Everyone deplores the attacks, but no one opposes them. George Khleifi, who runs the educational channel in Jerusalem, expresses similar ambiguities : " What can we say to these young people, who are willing to sacrifice their lives ? All they see is their parents' humiliation day after day ; they know Israeli soldiers can do whatever they want. There's no future for them. Most are desperate. I don't approve their acts, but I can understand them. " George Khleifi hints that the " resistance work " is shared between the enlightened bourgeois of the cities, who formulate political solutions, and the young in the camps, who provide the muscle.

The week has its lot of bad news : Sunday, a bombing raid against Syria, the tightening of the cordon around Nablus and Jenin, the near total closure of all checkpoints ; Wednesday and Thursday, the sealing of the access to Bir Zeit University, all classes cancelled ; Friday, a massive attack on Rafah in the south of Gaza. The Israelis pound the tunnels that run under the Egyptian border. " Everyone knows the tunnels exist ", says Shami, but more marijuana goes through than weapons. If the refugee camps were as well armed as the Israelis claim, their army would suffer many more casualties. "

The week has its unexpected lighter moments. Monday, Selim Quatab asks if his girlfriend, Reem, can occupy one of the vacant bedrooms in my flat. " You'll see. She's very neat and tidy. She's a student in sociology. Her family lives in a village. Given our customs I can't put her up in my place. " How can I say no ? Alerted on her mobile phone, Reem (" Gazelle " in Arabic) arrives moments later, a cute twenty-year-old brunette in jeans. If Mrs Huda accepts and they agree a price, I have no reason to object.

The next day I realise the error of my ways. The young " gazelle " is no student ; she has no books, not even a pen. Slouched in a chair in my living room, she watches schmaltzy video clips on Arab TV for hours on end. She dolls herself up, fiddles with her hair, lies around talking on the phone (on my phone). What she likes most, she explains seriously, is to sing, dance, swim and go horse-back riding in Jericho. My phone never stops ringing : Selim wants to talk to her. Sorry, she's in my shower. Sorry, she's not here. Sorry, I don't know where she is. Reem not only disturbs my concentration, the charming thing drives Selim up the wall too ; and he takes it out on my phone. The next time he rings I mutter a few unpleasantries in the mouthpiece.

The following afternoon, I find her in the company of a girlfriend and her two small children. The whole brood has been invited over for a bath in my bathroom. If all her friends and their brats come over to my place, good-bye tranquillity. I might as well look for an office downtown. Together I curse the " Gazelle ", her lump-head admirer and my own incorrigible silliness. The whole scene recalls the wonderful Turkish film Uzak, the story of a photographer whose quiet life of a bourgeois artist in Istanbul is disrupted by the arrival of a cousin from his village ; the visit, initially planned for a few days, stretches into weeks.

Let's take the situation with a little philosophy : I wanted to meet some Palestinians ; now they have come to me. It's their turn to stare at me dumbfounded. Why look any further ? All I have to do is spend my days watching Reem and Selim in their sentimental throes. I wanted to understand what it is like to be colonised ? Now I know !

Since Thursday evening the melodrama has become an opera. Poor Reem coughs worse than the Traviata. Selim, at her bedside, applies cool compresses to her forehead and spoon feeds her broth. I doubt he will win her heart this way. Then I wonder : is this sudden attack of illness the real thing ? Or is it staged for Selim's benefit ? Indeed for mine ?

Sunday afternoon. I hear loud explosions from the direction of the Muqataa. " It's nothing ", says my neighbour Majid, " just shots to intimidate ". Monday evening, around seven, Darwich Rish and I are talking cinema when gun shots go off nearby. Darwich, who makes action films, is familiar with such sounds. Looking over the balcony he says : " It's nothing. Just some kids having fun. " An hour later we hear the news : the Israelis have just arrested a PFLP[*] militant in a car with four others at the corner of Al-Manara Square. During the night from Thursday to Friday. We hear planes low over the city. In the morning rumour has it they were F16s on patrol. Who knows ? To be sure, it's best to read the newspapers and agency dispatches on the Internet.

---

[*] Popular Front for the Liberation of Palestine

To introduce this chronicle I need to go back to an insinuation I made earlier concerning the illness of my young flatmate, Reem. Her illness was in no way staged. I caught the virus too and have spent the last three days in bed shivering with fever and coughing until my chest aches. That will teach me to cast aspersions. Since getting back on her feet (I'm still bedridden), Reem has simply disappeared, leaving all her belongings in the room. To be continued.

Allow me, dear reader, a further remark to clarify my method. Not entirely deliberately, I have until now described directly what I see and hear, no more, no less. I intend to continue in this vein, inviting my reader to turn to the media for the usual news on the forming of a new Palestinian government, the construction of the wall (which I have not yet been to see), the hundred twenty-five buildings destroyed in Rafah and their twelve hundred occupants thrown into the street, the American veto against the recent UN Security Council resolution, the killing of three

American agents in Gaza, the new peace proposal tabled in Geneva ; in short all the issues, on which everyone, of course, has an opinion.

Many of the families, who settled in Ramallah after 1948, originated in Jaffa. Contrary to what orange juice drinkers might think, Jaffa was not an overly large orange grove. Darwich, my filmmaker friend, has a talent for bringing back to life the old Jaffa. He was born in the Amari refugee camp near Ramallah forty-five years ago and spent six years in Moscow studying filmmaking. We speak mostly English together, unless he can't find his words, then we switch to Russian. His flat, I tell him, with its outmoded furniture and antediluvian water closet could be Soviet-era. He agrees but adds it is hardly his fault if he spends his whole life in casual over-night accommodations. What he likes about Ramallah : " Today it is one of the most cosmopolitan places in the Near East, another Beirut. Like Jaffa in the old days. "

Jaffa is his paradise lost. His grandfather owned two horses and a cart that he used to haul goods between the port and the city, a useful profession. He was a man who enjoyed a little fun with his wealthier friends. As a child Darwich listened to his grandfather's stories about his youth in Jaffa, the orange blossoms, the irresistible call of the sea, the feverish nights at the port. Back then Jaffa was a city of mixed cultures. Even more than in Beirut and Alexandria, people laughed, played, invented, cheated, cried, sang and sighed in every language. " It was in Jaffa, in 1921 ", adds Darwich, " that the Lama (short for Salama) brothers produced the first Egyptian films. They were born in Argentina but came

28

originally from Bethlehem. Soad Hosny, the great movie star, the Cinderella of Egyptian cinema, was also a Palestinian from Jaffa – she died in London in 2001. "

From his grandfather Darwich inherited his love of swimming in the sea. But since the second Intifada three years ago, swimming has become impossible, even in the nearby Dead Sea. " If the religious Jews hold so dearly to their Holy Places, let them have the West Bank with Hebron and Jericho ; just leave us the coast – they don't care about it anyway. At least we could go swimming and do some business again ! " He loves the sea so much that in recent years he has travelled to Syria, Egypt and Tunisia. What are the beaches like in Syria, I ask ? " Big and empty. Not like Aqaba on the Red Sea, so overcrowded that people literally sit on top of each other. "

As for orange groves, one has to go down to the plain to Jericho or Tulkarm to see them. Up here in Ramallah, a thousand metres high, only olive trees grow.

Has he ever seen Jaffa with his own eyes ? After studying filmmaking Darwich took a job installing sun-powered water-heaters on roofs in Tel-Aviv-Jaffa (the two cities have now merged) – " One has to eat ", he says. His boss descended from an old Jewish family from Jerusalem and spoke Arabic with a slight " Jerusalem accent ", but other than that, perfectly. Moshe (Mussa in Arabic) put Darwich in charge of a six-man crew of recent Jewish immigrants (four from Russia and two from Argentina). " Darwich, I want you to cut these guys down to size before they eat us alive. " That was in 1989, a by-gone age, when it was still possible for a Jew to be Arab, even more Arab than Jew.

Sunday. Emily Gayyad, sixty years old, invites me for afternoon tea. She is also from Jaffa, but left when she was still a child. Her three girls and two grandsons sit on the terrace. The curtains are closed on all four sides to protect us from the sun. The building is located half-way up a long staircase in a residential Christian neighbourhood in Ramallah.

As is so often the case when travelling, one comes hoping to satisfy one's curiosity, but it's the host who assails you with questions. I no sooner have time to make myself comfortable on Emily's settee than the cross-examination begins. " You go to church, don't you ? What ? You're not Christian ? But you pray, don't you ? What ? Never ? What do you mean you don't believe in God ? Who made this table ? these hands ? the people sitting in this room ? Nature ? That's impossible. Everything comes from our Creator and Judge who opens the doors of Paradise to us. What ! You don't believe in Him ? Then where does morality come from ? Why should I return the ring I was given for safekeeping three years ago if God doesn't exist ? Do you read the Bible ? We are the children of God and must obey His will. After fifteen years of marriage and five daughters, God finally granted me a son, my Slimane (Solomon). I spent an entire night on my knees, on the cold floor, praying and begging. And God answered me. He healed my hands, too. My fingers were worn to the bone from washing, six were bleeding constantly. I prayed to God and again He healed me. "

In Ramallah Emily attended a well known school for girls, Saint Joseph of the Apparition. Proudly she remembers her spelling and grammar lessons, and of course the prayers and hymns in French and English. From a chain around her neck a diamond-incrusted cross hangs pertly on her silk blouse. She has put on make-up and done up her curly white hair for my visit.

Bustling with energy, she disappears into the kitchen and comes back with coffee and a plate of home-made almond fondants. (I dare not count the cakes I have eaten since arriving in Ramallah !) " Do you like them ? But you haven't tried that one. " She invites me to come back during Ramadan to taste her other specialties. Yet she cannot stomach the fact that I do not attend a single religious service. At the Orthodox Church in Ramallah, she explains, prayers are in Arabic ; no more than three words are in Greek. She is proud to be Arab and Middle Eastern. She pities us in the West because we have no family, no morality. As far as she is concerned, we live in hopeless isolation ; we don't even talk to our neighbours. Once she visited one of her daughters, who now lives in the United States, and realised the horror of Western life. She cannot understand why we in the West are so mistrustful of the Arabs. Only because she is Palestinian, the customs officer at Amsterdam airport asked her one rude question after another. The sainted soul has yet to recover from the experience.

Emily's three daughters – all university graduates (two are teachers, the third a civil engineer) – are horror-stricken at my lack of interest in God and His manifestations in the world. What a pity ! The eldest, a mathematics teacher, shows signs of an open mind : " Well, it's your right to think that way. But I do feel sorry for you ! " During our conversation the two young boys, eight and six years old, are seated at a table doing their school work. From time to time they sneak a look at their mothers. In Ramallah, Sunday like Friday is a day off, satisfying the sensibilities of all religious communities. Slimane, the beautiful baby boy who made his mother so happy, has just come in and takes a seat next to her. He is a strapping young man, twenty-two years old, jet black hair, a law student and member of the university basketball team.

" How did it go last year during the siege ? " I ask.

" Well, like everybody, we were pretty much locked up for five weeks, thirty-four days to be precise. It was really hard for little kids ; they weren't even allowed to go outside and play in the courtyard.

" Soldiers came to the house three times and searched everything. Once they ransacked our kitchen supplies, threw everything on the floor : flour, sugar, rice, pasta, tea, then mixed it up and urinated all over the mess. "

Two hours later I tear myself away from the hospitality of the Gayyad household. Showing me to the door, Emily takes my arm and says, " I will pray for you this evening. "

Tuesday. I have an appointment with Salam Hamdan, director of the Centre for Gender Studies at Al-Quds University (East Jerusalem). We meet after her lecture and go to her office. Gender studies as a discipline, she explains, is less concerned with women and more with the way gender differences work in society, politics and culture. Her first-year lecture is open to students regardless of major and is called " gender relations in the context of religion and society ". She begins the lecture every year with the same question : " What do you know about the West ? " Unfailingly, male and female students give the same answer : " It's the rule of individualism ; family members don't help each other ; everyone lives in isolation ; children don't have fathers ; Westerners have no morality. " – " What do you mean by morality ? " – " Well, they'll go to bed with anybody. "

The students seem to share the same prejudices as Emily. But are their prejudices any more outlandish than the prejudices we hold in the West about them ?

In her lectures Salam Hamdan tries to show that the rules defining gender roles in the family and in society owe everything to patriarchal structures, virtually nothing to religion. I ask if she has read Germaine Tillion, The Harem and the Cousins for example ? No, she is not familiar with Tillion's work. (Salam's university background is more Anglo-American.) She frequently faces opposition from Hamas students ; but students in general seem to have misgivings, at least until the end of the first quarter.

Salam Hamdan is not easily flustered. Jet-black cropped hair, big dark eyes ringed with kohl in Eastern Mediterranean style, wearing an exquisitely tailored outfit, she gives the impression of unbridled self-confidence. Salam is the daughter of a former communist party leader and is herself an ex-communist. She studied genetics in Prague and social science in Germany. Divorced from her husband (" still a good friend " spoken with a wry smile), she has a twelve-year-old daughter, Luna. Salam's secular upbringing, which she is now giving to Luna, was far from typical in Palestine, and certainly not representative. – " Given our manner of dress and behaviour, our neighbours thought we were

Christians ". In her teaching she tries hard to transmit values of tolerance, but the Islamists create more obstacles here than at Bir Zeit. " Maybe we can't fight for a secular state, but at least we can defend the idea that civil laws have priority over religious laws. "

" Do you discuss issues like bridal virginity in your classroom, or is this taboo ? " – If I did, I'd be finished. What I can do is fight against early marriage. – What about birth control ? – We discuss it, indirectly. Anyway, secular and religious leaders both agree on one issue : their policy is to encourage as many births as possible, for the " struggle ". But if we limit the number of early marriages, birth rates will drop automatically.

Salam Hamdan is currently campaigning with a feminist group for greater involvement of women in all aspects of Palestine's political life and institutions. " For a long time we thought our own demands as women would be addressed once national liberation was achieved. In other words, we wouldn't demand our own liberation until our country was free. Today our reasoning has changed. The plight of Algerian women after 1962 gave us an example not to be followed : after fighting for liberation alongside their men, they were sent back to their kitchens. That is what we don't want here. " She concludes, " In my opinion Hamas is even more dangerous than Ariel Sharon. " She is the second women to make the point this week. " Before the first Intifada, Hamas was virtually non-existent ; then Sharon systematically encouraged the movement. "

Judging by the number of educated women I have met since arriving in Ramallah – teachers, leaders of associations, directors of NGOs and heads of university departments – it's naïve to think that Palestinian women will go back to their kitchens. Then again, I forget we live in reactionary times.

Thursday. I have a meeting in the Shu'fat refugee camp with more women. These are women " in the field ".

I should say a few words about the " field ", or what is left of it. There are two checkpoints between Ramallah and Shu'fat. Before reaching Kalandia one gets the impression that something is gravely wrong. Suddenly the road becomes rough ; rubbish and filth pile up ; shops are dusty and dirty, most appear to be abandoned, windows broken. The collective taxi stops a hundred metres short of the checkpoint. Concrete blocks form a ring where Palestinians queue. Sometimes five minutes, sometimes two hours ; sometimes for nothing. Under the current clampdown there seems to be no sense in even trying : today only thirty people wait ; " normally " there would be several thousand. The Israeli soldiers wear heavy bullet-proof vests over their green uniforms. (In fact, it is the Palestinian civilians who would need such protection.) People on foot stop at one soldier, move on to the next, then reach an " office " – really just a plank of wood – where they present their IDs and personal belongings. Checking documents, the soldiers never utter a word. Permission to pass depends on official instructions, which are as erratic as the circumstances and depend on the mood of the duty officer.

On the opposite side of the checkpoint lorries queue to cross into occupied Palestine. The driver of a cattle lorry explains good-naturedly that he hopes to make it across in less than forty minutes. Only Israeli lorries – recognisable by their yellow number plates – circulate on both sides of the checkpoint ; lorries from Ramallah are not even allowed to travel to Jenin or Nablus.

To reach Shu'fat we climb aboard a second taxi and drive to another checkpoint. We walk across, take a third taxi, then a fourth...After five taxis I finally reach Shu'fat, eight kilometres from Ramallah. This densely populated area has collapsed into chaos under the devastating impact of colonisation. The Palestinian towns and villages on the outskirts of Jerusalem are physically cut off from one another by checkpoints and barbed wire, the lifeline to the city centre severed. In the collective taxi the silence is gloomy. The contrast with the friendliness of Ramallah is striking. Here the occupation is omnipresent ; life is carried out under the boot of the oppressor. I'm travelling without a compass or a map, but what does it matter ? No map shows the most recent checkpoints anyway. Like everyone else here, when I need information I rely on taxi drivers or word of mouth.

The Shu'fat refugee camp has some twenty two thousand residents. It gives the impression of a shantytown, an oversized village, a transit camp, a ghetto. Like so many poor Mediterranean villages it has narrow hillside streets lined with grocery stores, workshops, hairdressers and cafés, where men while away the hours. Laundry hangs from windows ; pipes and electrical wires mushroom anarchically. But unlike a shantytown, the streets are paved. There are public sewers and running water, and no more stray cats than anywhere else. Building quality is not on a par with council flats and living space is at a premium ; in fact, occupancy rates are high (three people to a room).

There are no parks or green spaces. Shu'fat's residents were driven out of the old city of Jerusalem during the Six Day War (1967). Little by little they built permanent houses, using mediocre material and following the original alignment of the refugee tents. The UNRWA[*] schools and dispensaries provide good quality schools and health services for the whole refugee population. But more than poverty, what strikes the eye is the population density and the total confinement. Barbed-wire fences carve up the horizon in every direction. The buildings beyond the fences, outside the camp, have white-stone facades that look almost luxurious in comparison.

Jihad Abu Znead is the director of the House of Women. In her office a small painting hangs on the wall given to her by friends from France. " We are twinned with Mantes-la-Jolie ", she explains between two phone calls. Her three cell phones never stop ringing. She has three in order to communicate with different regions of Israel and the Occupied Territories. Each works on a different band width (why make things easy ?). A stream of joyous female faces files through her office ; conversation is constantly interrupted. " This house was designed as the one place in the camp where the needs of women can be addressed. Except for school and their homes, there is simply no place for women to go. No doubt you saw the plaque at the entrance, so you know these facilities were built in 1997 with German government assistance. We provide as many services as possible in

---

[*] UNRWA (United Nations Relief and Work Agency for Palestine Refugees in the Near East) is responsible for the four million registered refugees in the West Bank, Gaza, the Lebanon, Syria and Jordan. Most of its twenty-two thousand employees (teachers and health workers) are themselves refugees.

the tiny space available to us. We have a multi-purpose hall with cooking facilities, a computer room, a beauty salon, a nursery and a kindergarten for one hundred twenty children. In all twenty-four women work here. " This pilot scheme gives Jihad a sense of accomplishment and pride. Other camps have developed similar projects and are networked together. This probably explains why she only has time for a cup of tea and a whirlwind tour of the facilities.

Every service that Jihad listed exists here in tiny miniature. The beauty salon, barely eight metres square, is packed with at least twenty women ; it is a hive of shampooed hair and rollers. A woman with short hair dyed a strange reddish colour stands out as the instructor. As for the kindergarten classes, they are microscopic too, especially given the number of children. Young boys and girls sit on the floor elbow to elbow. They wear the blue and white striped blouses typical of school children in Palestine. Wherever we go we are greeted by radiant smiles.

" The House of Women is planning an extension. The new building, already under construction, will house a covered swimming pool and a library. The only obstacle to completion is a demolition order issued by the Israelis ; construction work has been halted pending a court decision. " May Sa, a young woman in charge of information on drug addictions, is my new guide. As we tour the facilities we are followed by a group of giggling primary school girls.

Elegant, refined, May Sa has artfully tied two headscarves together to match the colours of her long silk skirt. From a well-to-do family she studied psychology and education. She does not live in the camp but comes here to work.

" How long have you worn a headscarf ? – Three years. – Since the start of the second Intifada ? – Yes, but that's not the reason. – For religious reasons ? – No, not really. Actually, I'm not very religious. – Because your family tells you to ? – No. My sister doesn't wear a scarf. I do it because I'm Palestinian. If I were Indian, I'd wear a sari. Where's the problem ? "

Like everybody else here, after the second war in Iraq, May Sa switched from Marlboro to Gauloises cigarettes. " The trouble is Gauloises have tripled in price. " She hopes to obtain a scholarship to finish her studies abroad, " maybe in Greece ". She has no plans to get married until she is at least thirty. In the meantime she will " live her life " the way she wants. Her light heartedness and warmth make me forget briefly the bleak sadness of the surroundings.

Back in Ramallah I am tempted to try one of the beauty parlours. I follow signs randomly in the high street until I find Yelena's salon. A native of the Ukraine, she welcomes the opportunity to speak Russian and tells me her story, as she pampers me with soothing facials and neck massages. Married to a Palestinian who, ten years ago, had gone to Kiev on a training course for technicians, she is mother to three young daughters. When she changed country, she also changed profession ; once a nurse, Now, after a training course in Tel Aviv, she is a beautician. " Life in the Ukraine is better. There's nothing to do here ; we are constantly hassled. My daughters want to go back. Last Tuesday the Israelis held another night-time raid ; they barged in at two a.m. Their faces painted black and green, green scarves on their heads. Fifty of them cordoned off the building. Just to control IDs. They do this all the time. And because of that, people here are becoming mean. They have been waiting for fifty-five years and each year it gets worse. I've lost faith, but I can't stop my husband from hoping. It's his country. "

A few more comments heard throughout the week.

" What really surprises me is that everybody here hasn't already become fascist. " Darwich.

" The Israelis complain that we don't like them. If only they'd give us one reason to like them ! " Souad.

" Once we have our Palestinian state we'll become an Arab state like every other, and it won't be as exciting. " Sally.

" If the good Lord really wants to do something for us, why doesn't he just get rid of Ariel Sharon and Yasser Arafat ? Those old fogies will never find a way out of this mess. Worse, they're starting to behave like a squabbling old couple. " Darwich.

" We don't need an historical leader anymore. We need a normal political leader that we can get rid of if he does a lousy job. " Sally.

" Oh, sure, the Israelis want me to work for them, but only as some sort of country constable. " Shami.

" One day the Israelis will have to admit that their State was born in sin. But even a child born in sin has a right to be loved and to go to school. " Souad.

Since the attack in Haifa the name Hanadi Jaradat is on everyone's tongue. She is the young lawyer who killed herself in revenge for the deaths of her fiancé and brother. Details of her story gradually emerge in the press. People sympathise with her and have pity.

May Sa tells me that the six women, who died in attacks so far, were all university graduates. She would like to study their motivations. I point out that without Islamic Jihad the young woman would not have killed. It might be better to investigate where the strategy is leading. May be, she says, then returns to the latest suicide bomber's psychological motivation. Is this what the expression " Palestinian Street " means, a raw emotional reaction to suffering and humiliation ?

Suicide bombings ? Liza Tamari starts : " People ask why we kill ourselves ? What else are we to do ? We've tried everything in the past fifty-five years : armed resistance, mass uprisings, negotiations. What is the outcome ? Just a tragic dead-end. Today people either turn to God or to suicide. What do you suggest ? " Liza, thirty years old, a university lecturer, speaks perfect French (she often travels to France for her research in the field of documentation and information systems). Her husband, a big kind man with blue eyes, is an architect. They have two young daughters (three years and eight months). Liza's life is about as ordered and comfortable as possible given the circumstances here. They live in a large, modern flat decorated in contemporary style without a hint of Middle Eastern influence. " My husband designed the furniture and chose the colours. " The bay window opens onto an immense panorama of semi-arid, rock-strewn hills. The only dark spot on the horizon, towards the north and east, is the blight of the Surda checkpoint : a tangle of yellow taxis, horse-drawn carts and scurrying pedestrians. The whole " pitiful mess " can be seen from Liza's balcony. The only way they can ignore it is to close the large yellow curtains and direct their gaze inward to a portrait of domestic bliss. Seated on a large yellow sofa, Liza is breast-feeding her youngest daughter, while her husband plays with the eldest. " She is allergic to cow's milk, so I must breast-feed her. " Her daughter feeds with determination. This tableau of modern maternity surprises. This slender mother in tight jeans, brunette with large black eyes and a wide warm smile, moves with elegance and grace. Difficult to picture despair behind such features. Liza insists, " Despair is all that is left here for us. "

She recalls nostalgically the first Intifada, when the Palestinian people took its struggle and daily survival into its own hands, helped by hundreds of organisations. But after the Oslo Accords and the creation of the Palestinian Authority these popular

42

initiatives all but disappeared. Since 2000 the harshness of the occupation leaves everyone struggling. What does she think about the Geneva Understandings currently being discussed ? Liza does not know the details, but she is not very enthusiastic. " There have been so many negotiations. What have they achieved ? And these leftwing Israelis, just who do they represent anyway ? "

Talking with Raed Andoni, a thirty-four-year-old documentary film producer, again the conversation turns to the suicide attacks : " We fight to live, not to die. Even Che Guevara's struggle was for life, not death. If we find death in battle, that's different. Today these operations reveal the desperation of our situation. We weren't in such dire straights at the time of the first Intifada. "

For the interview Raed Andoni recommends Stones, one of the trendy bars. Clips of Western singers performing their latest hits fill a wide screen. Soft music. Same for the lights. Sitting at tables, most of the patrons are young, male, only a few women. Everybody is drinking the local beer, Taibeh. I remark that the atmosphere is very Western. Raed objects, " There are places like this everywhere in Jordan, Egypt and Dubai. I can even show you pictures of my grandmother in the 1930s wearing a mini-skirt and low-cut blouse. " Maybe, but the women at the table next to us are obviously foreign.

Raed, like Liza, expresses regret for the by-gone days of the early 1990s, when political activism was lively and brotherhood was genuine. Regarding the Oslo Accords he is very critical. " Arafat wronged us with his negotiations. The Peace Process simply fragmented our fate as Palestinians, dividing us according to where we live, and whether we live inside or outside the Territories. The rights of one million Palestinians living inside Israel were simply ignored ; now they must fend for themselves. The fate of Palestinians outside the West Bank and Gaza – the four hundred thousand in Lebanon and the other four hundred thousand in Syria – has been neglected too. Dividing the Territories into three zones – Zone A, B and C.[*] – means that Palestinians no longer share the same status. The Israelis have issued different IDs for each town, so now when we reach a checkpoint, all we do is try to get through without regard for our fellow Palestinians. It's a huge step backward. About the only thing the Peace Process has achieved is to weaken the Palestinian side. We were given a little king with his courtiers and in the meantime the Israelis have increased their stranglehold. What we need is a statesman, not short-sighted politicians. The only one who had any vision of the future was the late Edward Said. "

During the first Intifada Raed was an activist in a left wing political organisation. He received his political education in prison. " I was a twenty-year-old student. I was arrested at home with a forbidden book. One year in prison is really a short sentence here. From the moment you're arrested until the moment you pass through the prison gates they do everything to break you physically and psychologically. But once you're in prison, the political organisations take charge of your life. Hamas didn't exist at the time. There was only Islamic Jihad, PFLP and above all

---

[*] Zone A, urban areas under the control of the Palestinian Authority ; Zone B, areas under shared control ; Zone C, areas exclusively under Israeli control.

44

Fatah. Our lives were regimented by these organisations from dawn to dusk. We read for two hours in the morning, then took an hour of physical exercise in the yard. There were discussions about ideology, history, and economics ; it was in prison that I read Marx and Lenin – and novels too. It was my job to wash the corridors, where I learned to deliver messages. I became a very good cleaner ; it's a useful skill. "

Raed does not believe in a two-state solution. He is not the first to share his doubts with me. " With their policy of fait accompli the Israelis are just absorbing us within their own borders. With each day that goes by, the creation of a Palestinian State on a tiny territory becomes less and less likely. So, for us, the only option is to resist and to struggle for our rights within this 'Greater Israel'. "

Raed concludes : " In the long run who needs either a Jewish state or a Palestinian state ? What is needed is a state for everybody in this country, a state that grants equal rights to all. "

Maybe the two-state solution should be seen as a transition phase before the creation of a single dual-national state ? " Edward Said came round to this same conclusion near the end of his life. If we have to go down this route, because the Jews need a state with a Jewish majority, then so be it. But, personally, I believe less and less in such a solution. "

" I hope you won't throw yourself out the window if I am too frank in giving my opinion about a two-state solution " warns Inam, professor of media studies and journalism. It's lunchtime in the cafeteria of Bir Zeit University. I have been chatting with this highly strung young woman in blue jeans ever since she finished her lecture over an hour ago. She is in great need of unwinding.

" Why should we pay for the persecutions of the Jews in Europe ? We had nothing to do with it. Why should we sacrifice our land ? Let the Europeans pay if they want to make reparations. – Don't worry, Inam, I won't throw myself out the window, but your attitude implies continuing the struggle until Israel disappears completely. Don't you think it's better to put an end to the war ? – But why should we be the ones to surrender our rights ? We have resisted for fifty-four years. We won't leave this place and we will continue to resist because our cause is just. "

Inam, Raed, May Sa, Liza, extremists ? Far from it. Not an ounce of radical Islamism in their veins. A recognised place in Palestinian society, university graduates, gainfully employed, relatively prosperous. So ? Frustration that concessions are never matched ? A desire to end the long historical struggle in genuine victory rather than in semi defeat (a rump state governing twenty-two percent of Palestinian territory) ? A need for revenge for the suffering and humiliation ?

Inam is not the first to mention the Holocaust, the term used here (Shoah is the term used in Israel). Not the first to accuse Europeans of acquitting themselves of their debt to the Jews by dumping them on the Middle East, abusing their colonial position. But Inam is the first person I meet to put Holocaust denial in a positive light. I still do not throw myself out the window, but strongly object to her negationism. She defends herself, " But I wasn't aware that the historians simply denied the existence of gas chambers. I thought they were contesting the number of victims and the political capital being made. " Sadly not. Inam is a well-travelled intellectual ; she studied filmmaking in France and Egypt. I am dismayed to see her join forces with the enemies of her enemies so quickly. Such an attitude is common and always disquieting. In Palestine, people snatch at any argument that comes to hand for better or worse.

On the other hand, some surprise me with an uncanny freedom of tone in their speech. Sari Hanafi, director of a research centre on Palestinian refugees, is one of these. He earned his doctorate in sociology in Paris. A few minutes into our conversation he quotes Hannah Arendt, whom he reads admiringly. I take to him immediately. In his research and public debates Sari Hanafi digs into issues that are taboo. Rather than focus on the memory of a lost homeland, like most of his colleagues, Sari studies the adaptation of refugees to the new economic and cultural environment in the Lebanon and Jordan. He also pursues a keen interest in the concrete application of a " right of return " and attempts to ensure that the issue is dealt with pragmatically. " Symbolically a " right of return " has to be granted to every Palestinian ; which is to say, Israel must recognise its responsibility in the exodus and suffering of all Palestinians since 1948. Something it has never done. Offering Palestinians the opportunity to return to their pre-1948 homes and fields will not involve mass population movements. Palestinian refugees have always cherished the dream of return, but there are other options : settlement within the new Palestinian state, permanent residence in the country of adoption. But it will not be possible to explore these options seriously until the issue of despoliation is officially recognised and until the right of reparation is fully accepted. When similar cases of displaced populations around the world are examined – for instance the case of Ireland – it becomes clear that after a long period of absence the effective rate of return is always extremely low. This should be reassuring for the Israelis.

Tuesday. Malika is back from Lebanon where she participated in an academic conference. Exhausted by long delays at the Allenby Bridge crossing and disgusted by the attitude of the Jordanian border police – " worse than the Israelis " – she goes straight to the doctor with serious symptoms of stress and depression. She cries for every reason and no reason ; she aches everywhere ; she can't concentrate. Yesterday her physiotherapist spent the day relaxing and consoling her. Malika is not a delicate nature by any means ; she is, in fact, the pillar of the social science department at Bir Zeit University. An ex-communist, a committed feminist, she is a popular figure in Ramallah ; warm and hospitable, her house is always open to female friends and students, who also become her friends. Malika took me under her wing as soon as I arrived, but now it is she who needs moral support. When we walk to the campus together, it is I who carry her briefcase. We plan to relax in the hamam after her lecture. But today everything goes wrong ; she quarrels with her mother, who is as helpless as a babe ; she accuses the hamam owner of exploiting her masseuse, whom she underpays. Her mother endures her daughter's sullenness, but the hamam owner answers back with insolence. The squabble degenerates and, exasperated, Malika angrily stomps out of the hamam.

A few minutes later I am in the steam bath with Irina, Malika's strapping sister-in-law. A mid-wife by profession, Irina comes from Rostov-on-Don, where thirty years ago she met her husband. He is a well-known Palestinian doctor and Malika's brother. Our conversation takes place in Russian because Irina, with all these events, never found time to learn English, nor I to learn Arabic. Soon we are comparing the merits of baths in Russia and Palestine. In Russia the steam is perfumed with eucalyptus leaves ; Birch tree twigs are used for whisking the body. In Palestine the dominant fragrance is Spearmint and the bather uses a cotton washcloth. In Russia bathing is in the nude, here a swimsuit is necessary. The setting is different as well. In Russia, in the villages at least, the steam room is installed in a wooden bathhouse at the back of the garden. Here everything is made of marble. Irina remains Russian ; in her mind nothing can ever replace the bathhouses of her homeland. She tells me this and many other stories (some are downright depressing), as she scrubs my back. In turn I scrub this lusty blond until we are both as red as lobsters. In Ramallah, I am told, there is an association of Russian or Russian-speaking women with over four hundred members, who are married to Palestinians.

Meanwhile night has fallen : Malika and I are scouring the streets of Ramallah in search of a grand hotel hosting a cultural event for the French poet Francis Combes. Just as we arrive in a room overflowing with officials from the French Consulate and the Palestinian Authority, curfew is declared. Israeli tanks rumble into the city.

Malika hustles me back into her small automobile : " All we have to do is stay off certain streets and we'll get through. " The scene is amazing. In no time the streets of the city centre have emptied, the shops have pulled down their shutters and the only people walking in the night are a few empty-handed young men. They are hurrying back from Al-Manara Square where the Israeli tanks seem to be taking up positions. We hear explosions and smell tear gas. Malika, heedless of warnings from taxi drivers, threads her way through the city centre frequently the wrong way down one-way streets. We finally make it back to her place. What a relief! But no sooner do we arrive than the phone rings : Faroun, Malika's nephew, is home alone on the opposite side of the city, and he is frightened. He calls his aunt to the rescue. I won't let her make the trip alone. Despite the curfew we get back into the car and set out to fetch Faroun, taking care to stay off the main streets. Suddenly Malika pulls to the side of the road as two armoured vehicles with wire-protected windows rumble past. They make a toad-like sound. Faroun is waiting for us by the gate. He jumps into the car, looks nervously for his cell phone and finds it. " The problem with curfews is that bread disappears from the bakeries in no time. But don't worry ; I have everything to make some at home. " Anyway Malika makes two or three stops at grocery stores just in case…The atmosphere in the stores is strange : shoppers crack jokes as they make last-minute purchases. People share the latest news. Are we headed for a twenty-four hour curfew or will it last a month ? " With the Israelis anything can happen. But one thing is certain, tomorrow access to the university will be impossible. I'm so exhausted ; I'm almost pleased. " More explosions and detonations in the distance. At the house our trio is met by three more visitors : Wilhelm, Peter and Tania (a visiting artist). We eat, drink and discuss politics, again swapping the latest news. The wine and whisky soon lift our voices to fever pitch. I begin to float in a wave of English and Arabic sounds. Through all the noise I hear Tania's voice : " I just had a call on my cell phone from an Israeli officer here in Ramallah. He's here on manoeuvres. He told me not to worry. Oh, you're probably surprised. I'm sorry. He's a former school friend ; we went to the same posh school in Jerusalem. And let me surprise you some more : my father and my cousin are Israeli policemen. I have radical ideas but the rest of my family stands firmly behind Israel. " In appearance Tania could hardly be more Arab-looking. She is lovely, dark-skinned with curly long black hair, a tall buxom young woman with a soft friendly smile. Her family is affiliated with the Maronite Church in Jerusalem. Malika, whose family is Orthodox (and communist), announces that she too has a cousin in the Israeli police : they once found themselves face-to-face in a demonstration and she told him in no uncertain words exactly what she thought of him.

Lovers of moving stories – with good guys and bad guys, the oppressed poor and the rich oppressor, the Arabs and the Jews, Easterners and Westerners – don't bother to read on ! What you find here are Arabs who collaborate with the enemy and Arabs who fight in the resistance, Eastern Jews (read Arabs) who prefer Arab Muslims to European Jews, Arab Christians and Arab Muslims who do not intermarry, Jewish families, at each other's throats, just like Arab families, who tear themselves apart too. A civil war, open or masked, rages at every level. The scepticism surrounding the two-state solution is comprehensible. How is it possible to separate something so incredibly entangled ? What could possibly justify an invisible border separating 1.2 million Arabs (Muslims and Christians), all Israeli citizens, from their cousins on the other side (3.7 million Palestinians in the Occupied Territories and over four million more in the Diaspora) ?

The rest of the evening at Malika's place is " among girls ". Tania changes the topic of conversation. " What I need in my life right now is a boyfriend. I have no one. " Such a beautiful woman and no male friends in her life, how is that possible ? I tell her so. " My mother warned me, if I bring back a non-Christian she'll break every bone in my body and wring my neck like a chicken. " Tania mimics her mother's gesture. " That seriously limits the playing field. Anyway I'm too free and independent for men here. The only man in my life that I almost had an affair with was a Frenchman in Paris. I was really attracted until I realised he was Jewish. Then it was out of the question. " Malika, too, almost had an affair with a Muslim. She was in her forties, still unmarried (nothing but " Platonic relationships " until then). When her father caught wind of something, he rushed home and cursed a blue streak. " And my father was very liberal, a communist ; he even campaigned for the mayor of Nazareth (do you remember, everybody hated him because he married a Muslim). " Tania continued, " When I was twenty I thought perhaps I would become a nun. I spent a year in a convent. What a nightmare ! Then I thought maybe I was a Lesbian ; so I spent another year in therapy. I even asked a girlfriend to undress in front of me to test my reaction. " Malika adds, " When I was young I also thought of entering a convent…Today I can say I'm probably eighty percent happy with my life, but I keep the door open, just in case. With everything we've been through, the Intifada, the occupation, the constant struggle, conditions weren't right for achieving personal happiness. "

Tania, twenty-eight years old, and Malika, fifty-four : two independent women who this evening meet each other for the first time. They get to know each other, then confided in one another frankly, spontaneously, with humour. Every utterance – their loneliness, the painful distance with men who are trapped in patriarchal roles – sounds familiar to me. The main difference between us : the severity of prohibitions and the oppression of families holding sway over everyone at every age. There is a suffocating obligation to transform every love affair into marriage, not just between two individuals, but between two entire families. Individual freedom remains confined to a narrow space.

Liza Tamari, whose immediate neighbours are her brothers-in-law and sisters-in-law, explains it like this : " The family is our national security system. The state is so weak, health and retirement systems almost non existent, insecurity so relentless that no one can make it without the family network. This may be a little less the case among the rich. Without retirement system, people are completely dependent on their sons in old age. Of course we argue and fight, but we need each other. Family life is traditional here and its an economic necessity. " Meanwhile, over the last thirty years, families have invested in the education of their daughters despite the complete lack of opportunity on the job market. The result : an immense hiatus for well-education young women who are married off at an early age (thirty percent before seventeen) and marched onto the path of family and patriotic reproduction (5.9 children per woman). To be continued.

Wednesday morning. The curfew is lifted. News circulates on what happened in the city centre last evening. Having lost three soldiers last Sunday, the Israelis swept into Ramallah with forty armoured vehicles to round up suspects. First the army went to the mosque to control identities. Outside in the street a young man was shot in the head. Married for only three weeks, he leaves a widow. In the words of my neighbour : " Yesterday the Israelis created another candidate for a suicide bombing. "

23 – 30 October

As the end of my first month in Ramallah draws near, I am increasingly choked by an anger that grabs me by the throat and strangles and suffocates me. Yesterday I flew into a rage because Christians, Jews and Muslims, who kill each other over the " Holy Lands ", are so absurdly sanctimonious. The day before, the Palestinian media provoked my ire because of their senseless justifications of " martyrdom operations ". As for how I feel when I pass by heavily fortified Jewish settlements protected by Israeli soldiers and serviced by fine paved roads – the kind that scar the beautiful landscape of Palestine – I tremble in anger. When I pass through a checkpoint and see the local residents as they trudge through the mud and kowtow to the occupier, somehow restraining their fury, I'm at a loss for words and prefer to keep my thoughts to myself.

A month ago I knew no Palestinians, had never met one. I had never read a Palestinian author, poet or thinker, except may be on the commentary page of a newspaper. I pictured life in occupied Palestine through whatever documentary films I had seen.

I did not come here in friendship for the Palestinian people : I didn't know any Palestinians. I was not motivated by sympathy : I knew nothing about the Arab world (I don't even speak Arabic). I feel no solidarity with the national liberation struggle ; I am genetically indifferent to nationalist claims. I came to see what the Jewish state is doing here, in the name of Jews around the world, i.e. in my name. I want to hear the other side of our story ; visit the dark side of our moon. I do this first of all for my own sake, to open my eyes. " I didn't know " has never been a valid excuse.

Since childhood I heard about " Arabs ", never " Palestinians ". My maternal grandmother, a committed Zionist, spent the second half of her life battling the enemies of Israel. She is buried less than fifteen kilometres from here, on the other side of Jerusalem. My father gave up the idea of settling in Israel (and bringing me into the world here). Yet, never a year went by without a visit to his boyhood friends from Germany and Alsace, now living in a Kibbutz, or to his countless relatives living in Israel. On this score, and for the sake of clarity, my parents met shortly after the war at a Zionist rally in London. Two thirds of my family back the Jewish state, more or less passionately. I am not an ordinary tourist here.

Tourism. I wanted to visit Nablus, forty miles to the north, one of the most beautiful Arab towns in the region. Last Thursday I undertook the trek – the word is not too strong – in the company of Rainer, a trainee teacher at the Goethe Institute. An athletic young man with a shock of blond hair, he stands out like a sore thumb in this country. He teaches a beginner's course in German to about twenty students at the university in Nablus. He has made the trip numerous times and knows all the pitfalls. We set out before seven a.m.. For two shekels the first collective taxi – called " service " on this side, " sherout " on the other – drops us at Kalandia, three kilometres to the south. The checkpoint has just opened and we cross – on foot naturally – without trouble. A second " service " (five shekels) takes us northeast to Taibeh checkpoint. The military roadblock, next to a small army fort flying an Israeli flag, sits at the intersection of two totally empty roads smack in the middle of a treeless plateau under a rising sun. It promises to be a warm day for this time of year (the forecast calls for thirty degrees Celsius). The soldiers pay little attention to our IDs. We cross two lengths of barbed wire and climb into another " service " three hundred metres further up the road. The diesel engine idles as the driver waits for all seven places to fill. There is no one coming from our direction, but on the opposite side scores of men – in jeans or suits, carrying bags or briefcases – follow trails through the scrub to avoid the checkpoint. The soldiers see them but make no attempt to stop them. The wait drags on. If Rainer and I agree to pay four times the going rate for the missing passengers, the driver will leave. We tell him fifteen shekels is expensive enough and we strike up a conversation as we wait in the middle of the desert plateau. The sun etches shadows between the rocks and clumps of bushes. The burly, half-bald driver tells us his woes in elementary English. He gestures to his balding pate, unbuttons his shirt, apologizing to me for his impudence, and reveals the hairs on his chest. Only forty years old, he laments, and the hairs are already white. He has four children but could only afford to send two to university. His youngest son sits at home bored while the others study. " No other people on earth have been treated the way the Jews treat us. First they killed Christ, now it's Mohammed. " In his diatribe he curses anyone who fails to stop or punish his oppressors, especially Americans. I tell him I don't agree – that confusing the issues will certainly not help. Rainer is unmoved by the tirade which, he says, is common among taxi drivers. Conversation tapers off. Three quarters of an hour later a group of strapping young men loom up from a desert trail. They are residents of the same village as our driver. After much hugging and kissing, they climb in. Nine fifteen. We finally leave the checkpoint area.

When we reach Taibeh the taxi stops outside a grocery store ; one of the passengers brings back a large bottle of orangeade, which he shares with all of us. Hospitality, always. Taibeh is a fair-sized Christian village, still quiet at this early morning hour. I see a few one and two storey buildings, their facades made of stone. There is a steeple and a few dusty stores. The taxi driver points out the village's famous brewery, the only one in the West Bank. The street is in poor repair. Huge mounds of earth have to be skirted by driving on the edge of the road. We rarely exceed forty kilometres per hour. After Taibeh the road follows a green, olive-dotted valley. Families of women and children work in the olive groves. Ramadan begins in two or three days and will make working in the fields very unpleasant. Farmers rush to finish their harvest while they can still work on full stomachs. Coming round a bend in the road the vista opens onto a broad slope of hundred-year old olive trees in tiered rows : " Home ", says the driver with pride.

At the top of the hill and to the right, a housing development with a hundred or so identical-looking structures appears. " Israeli settlers took our olive trees over there, to the right of the road. " Dropping off his Palestinian passengers, then struggling through the difficult portions of the road (obstacles, sleeping policemen, potholes), the taxi finally reaches the third checkpoint, Zatara. We get out and walk across an intersection which joins two wide and perfect roads (their signs are in Hebrew). For the third time today we show our passports to young Israeli soldiers – they look like high school kids – who ask us what we are doing here. One of the soldiers has written his name in marker on his helmet, Charlie Weizmann. Another looks at my passport and tells me – in English ! – he holds a French passport, too. Two hundred metres down the hill Palestinian taxis wait for their customers. Three more shekels.

A hundred metres from the Hawara roadblock all joking ends. Nablus, a major centre of the resistance movement, has been locked down for three years. Soldiers control the access points (rumour has they hail from the nearby settlements). Each time Rainer passes through Hawara he is exacerbated. Last week, soldiers trained their weapons on a thirteen-year-old boy and ordered him to collect the rubbish on the ground. Crossing through the checkpoint requires either a safe conduct, a diplomatic passport or pure luck. Rainer has a safe conduct, I rely on good fortune. The waiting crowd is dense, perhaps three hundred people in two separate queues, men on the left, women and children on the right. Here women are less elegant than in Ramallah : no makeup, no jeans, no high heels. In long coats touching their shoes, covered by snugly fastened headscarves, most perspire heavily in the sun. Older women, with large bundles on their heads, wear embroidered country dresses. It is ten o'clock and many have been waiting since dawn. The soldiers allow only ambulances through the checkpoint. Vans with red crosses on their sides will take passengers across for a fee (two hundred fifty shekels !). The soldiers appear to condone the practice ; do they share in the profits ?

Rainer and I quit the queue and approach the soldiers cautiously. He crosses without difficulty but I am stopped curtly by a small thick-set soldier. " No tourists allowed in Nablus ". I invent an appointment at the university and stand there, waiting for the big blond soldier with the phlegmatic face to finish with an old man in a traditional keffiyeh, who angrily shakes his cane and insists on his right to go back home. The blond soldier tells me in a weary voice, " There is no crossing here. If you go I can't guarantee your return. " I take it as a green light and set out slowly, fearful of a last-minute change of mind. I cover the final one hundred metres, then locate Rainer who has kept a seat for me in the minibus. It leaves immediately. What a relief !

The tally for the morning : twenty-eight shekels fifty spent, three hours forty wasted ; on a normal day, twelve shekels and forty-five minutes would have been plenty. Yet it is easy for Rainer and me ; we have foreign passports and hardly waited at any of the four checkpoints. Irina, the midwife I met the other evening, told me she recently travelled from Tulkarm to Jerusalem ; the trip took twelve hours and she crossed thirty five checkpoints.

The passenger next to us in the minibus is a young man in a business suit. During the conversation he shows us an unused plane ticket dated October fifteenth. A German association had invited him – all expenses paid – to attend a conference in Düsseldorf. Last week, he says, he set out for the international airport in Amman. At the Israeli border control on Allenby Bridge (the only possible exit point since Ben Gourion airport is closed to West Bank residents) a soldier turned him back, ironically telling him to try again next month after the commanding officer gets back from his holiday. The wasted ticket is still in his wallet. He hands us his business card : Yasser Alawneh, The Palestinian Independent Commission for Citizen's Rights, Nablus ". Since there are neither rights nor citizens here, I wonder what the members of this commission actually do.

Driving into Nablus is a shock. Gaping trenches, thick dust and filth can be seen everywhere. The snarl of yellow taxis is inextricable. With a population of nearly one hundred fifty thousand Nablus lies in a narrow valley hemmed in by steep hills. The lovely villas on the hill tops are a reminder that many of the local residents struck it rich in the Gulf (called here " Arabian "). The downtown area – with its big-city office buildings and shopping malls – is in an appalling state. Bombs have flattened or gutted numerous public and private buildings. In comparison, the university campus on the hill top is a mirror of luxury. I arrive at the campus in the footsteps of Rainer by midday.

Unlucky and lucky. I discover – unlucky – that Thursday is the first day of the weekend ; the other being Friday of course. In Ramallah the weekend is Friday and Sunday, while in Jordan it is Friday and Saturday. (My hosts here take the Jordanian Saturday rest day as a sign of connivance with the Israelis. Absolutely everything here is desperately political.) I won't meet many people on campus today, in any case not the colleagues of the French Department who have all left. The first person I speak to – lucky – is very courteous, a nuclear physicist called Zaid Qamhieh. Last month he was in Germany working on the particle accelerator in Darmstadt. " I have a friend in Paris in the same line of work ", I tell him. Forty, slender, serene, Zaid Qamhieh speaks English with a soft voice. He takes me to the office of Ala Yavied, the PR officer of Al-Najah International University. Everything in the building is clean, modest and empty. Ala Yavied is a professor of journalism and handles his job with aplomb. His visitor documentation is excellent. It not only provides information about the learning facilities on campus but also about the hardships that students face under Israeli occupation. There are statistics on the number of killed, wounded and imprisoned since 2000 as well as an impact analysis of the military siege in the spring of 2002. I am saddened by the drop in enrolment, from nine thousand five hundred in 2001 to seven thousand in 2003, owing primarily to travel restrictions between neighbouring townships but also to the increasing poverty of Palestinian families (tuition fees vary anywhere from six hundred to three thousand dollars per semester). " The right to study is a basic human right ", Ala Yavied states. Dense crowds of students hover around the university's three large lecture halls. " Our current facilities are overcrowded. Come back next year and you'll see our new campus. "

Students are leaving a hall at the end of a lecture sponsored by the Institute of Islamic Studies. Ala Yavied introduces me to a high-ranking theologian, who does not shake my hand but salutes me piously with hands on chest. Virtually every female student wears a scarf. I make the remark that the weight of Islam seems heavy here. " And where will it all lead you ? – To hell, " Ala Yavied replies, depressed. He grows nervous when I take out my camera. " We're fed up with journalists who come here to exaggerate the importance of radical Islamist groups, and those who collect information and post it on Israeli websites. " It is the first time I feel such reticence. Granted I have arrived unannounced and without a letter of recommendation in the office of this communication expert. This may explain his reservations. The professor of nuclear physics remains silent, his only concern is to help and to make a new contact ; we exchange addresses and phone numbers. " Because of the curfew and the closure, I have nothing to do here on my days off. There is no swimming pool, no entertainment. I just stay on campus and work. "

From a cultural point of view the old city of Nablus, once called " little Damascus ", is well worth a visit. Officially the bombing of the kasbah in April 2002 destroyed sixty buildings and damaged five hundred others (half of these are threatening to collapse). Despite the destruction, which left scores of dead and wounded in its wake (many buried under their houses), the souk continues to draw crowds.

There are furniture and clock repairmen, metal and leather workers, perfumers, tailors, bakers, fruit and vegetable stall keepers, spice vendors. Some rebuilding has begun. The Italians are financing repairs to a small Orthodox Church – its icons are exquisite – barely a hundred metres from the Al-Nasr mosque. A Japanese foundation is funding the restoration of an old soap factory. The day Palestine wriggles free from the economic blockade and begins its reconstruction, the kasbah will surely become a major tourist attraction again. Meanwhile the scene is heartbreaking. Vendors and children stare at me in surprise. There have been virtually no tourists for three years ; rarely a woman alone. They chant in unison " Welcome to Nablus " and it cheers me. Smiling, an older vendor replies to my enquiry : " Madam, it's my pleasure to assist. I admire your country. if I can help please come back anytime. " Despite all else, politeness has not suffered.

Incidentally, Israeli maps and road signs do not recognize Nablus. Its official name is the biblical Sichem. In general, place names are a bone of contention between Israel and Palestine. As far as Palestinians are concerned, this is the West Bank ; the Israelis call it Judea and Samaria. As for the term " Occupied Territories ", some find it more politically correct to reduce it to " Territories ". But what population has ever inhabited the land of " Territory " ?

The return journey to Ramallah is quicker ; the mood at the Hawara checkpoint buoyant. Turning the pages of my passport, the sentry queries " Happy now ? " I let the question pass. The passport of my German travel companion draws further unexpected commentary : " So, you're from Düsseldorf. My

64

grandmother comes from Cologne. " The presence of human rights observers at the checkpoint no doubt explains the friendly banter. A spanking new bus full of settlers captures everybody's attention as it drives through. A short while later traffic slowly returns to normal. Surprisingly, after Zatara the soldiers have opened the main road ; this means Kalandia is only thirty minutes away instead of three hours. The new four-lane highway serves only the Jewish settlements visible here and there on the hilltops. Each settlement has its own security post and is under armed guard by the occupants themselves. High tech barbed wire, satellite dishes and radar bristle everywhere ; security is clearly the priority here. The architecture reminds me of cheap tract housing. It is at odds with the Arab townships situated down in the valley below. On the opposite side of the road a bearded settler in a prayer shawl hitches a ride. Is there an Uzi in his rucksack ? What life (or non-life) is there in these fortresses that one can leave only under armed escort ? How can Israeli voters swallow the lie that settlers " spontaneously " occupy these outposts ? If the army withdrew its protection, life expectancy here would not exceed half an hour. This week a lone Palestinian gunman killed three Israeli soldiers (two of them women) defending the settlement of Netzarim in Gaza[*]. Last week three soldiers died in an ambush near the Ofra settlement. " How long will Israeli families accept the sacrifice of their children for the settlers ? " asks Uri Avnery in his weekly commentary. Most people believe it will take a lot more military

---

[*] Netzarim was evacuated and destroyed in August 2005 after the Israeli withdrawal from Gaza.

losses before any reaction sets in[*]. Blood and more blood. How fortunate, this is what the media crave.

Saturday. Twenty radical peace organisations from Israel join forces to organise an olive harvest in the Occupied Territories. Seven different buses leave Jerusalem, Tel-Aviv and Haifa early in the morning; they converge on the village of Hirbat Habara at ten o'clock sharp. Three hundred fifty volunteers unite to assist farmers whose groves are trapped between the Green Line and the new " security fence ". This wide swath of barbed wire in the middle of olive groves has made the Saleh family's existence a hell. In comparison, sporadic clashes with Israeli settlers appear almost trifling. In a blend of bureaucratic punctiliousness and brutality, the army has tried everything to push them off their land, beginning with the uprooting of sixty-five olive trees, to make way for the " fence " (Israel magnanimously returned the wood for heating). Today the Saleh family needs one permit to live on their land and another to enter the village or to work their groves located on the other side of the barbed wire. Abed Saleh's wife has been denied this second permit and, therefore, she is no longer able to assist her husband in the fields. Abed can cross over to his land, but he is not allowed to take his tractor. His sister-in-law is head mistress of the village school. Whether she reaches her office or not depends on the mood of the military. Morning and evening she passes through an electronic gate, the latest novelty in Israeli security technology. In

---

[*] Statistics for the period September 2000 to February 2008 show 326 Israeli security force personnel killed, of which 239 in the Occupied Territories (Source : B'Tselem, an Israeli human rights organisation monitoring the Occupied Territories).

principle, the guard comes on duty at seven a.m. ; in practice, he arrives when he feels like it. The same applies for ambulances, doctors, fire personnel...Of course, if the head mistress does not reach school on time, the children have to wait outside. Today's action is intended to back the Saleh family. The risk is that, like many others before them, they will abandon their ancestral lands if they can no longer work them.

The average age of Israeli activists at Hirbat Habara is around fifty, mostly women. Uri Avnery, the oldest person here, will give the closing speech. Throughout the day I talk with quite a few people. Even in this tiny circle of Israeli leftists, I can't get over the distance separating them from the other side. One woman laments, as she stands in front of the barbed wire fence, " If everyone in Israel could see this, they would sympathize ! " Another expresses shock when I say that the dream of many Palestinian youths is to kill an Israeli soldier. Another is worried that her son will lose his driving licence if he argues psychiatric illness to avoid military service. But what does he risk if he is assigned to protect a settlement in the middle of the West Bank ? And what do Palestinian civilians risk if they come across a terrified soldier at a checkpoint ? I prefer to remain silent. It's almost as if the word " occupation " has no precise meaning here. There is great confusion over the refugee issue as well. To this day the state of Israeli has not accepted responsibility for the mass exodus of Palestinians in 1948. The official version is they departed of their own free will and, in so doing, renounced their right of return – and their citizenship rights as well – in their own country. For Palestinians, whether refugees or not, whether candidates for return or not, the denial of the national tragedy is the greatest trauma. Israel's "new historians" have brought into full view the absurdity of this myth. Its politicians have yet to do so. As for the Geneva Understandings, it does not achieve a shared historical narrative. "That will be the next step", says another activist. How long do Israeli leftwing movements think they can preach patience to the Palestinians?

Saturday. Start of Ramadan. Most restaurants are closed during the daytime. From now on alcohol is sold under the counter, out of the sight of prying eyes. Bakers offer kataief, a pancake-like sweet stuffed with either cheese or a walnut and honey syrup. At five p.m. the streets empty in an instant and everyone rushes home to gorge on food with the family. At the top of his lungs the muezzin delivers his call to prayer amplified by a screeching microphone.

Sunday. Visit from Jean-Claude, a friend from Paris, who is building solidarity with the children's theatre in the Aida refugee camp near Bethlehem. Evening, official reception at the Muqataa with Yasser Arafat who hosts a French delegation : twenty-five delegates from municipalities in France twinned with Palestinian towns and cities. I mingle with my compatriots. Curiosity gets the better of me. The visitors are appalled at the dilapidation of the Presidential offices. The heap of gutted cars in the courtyard resembles a sculpture by Cesar. The sentry's box, assembled from the mortar and brick of the surrounding ruins, looks like a slum structure. It is unbelievable how lax security is. " Access here is like climbing onto a merry-go-round " says one of the old communist militants. An attempt on Arafat's life here would not tax the skills of a mediocre secret agent.

Half an hour later the President (rais in Arabic) appears among the guests dressed in his military khakis and legendary kaffiyeh. He seems rather healthy ; his face does not quiver. He makes the rounds, smiling and greeting every male visitor with a handshake, kissing every woman on the hand. A deputy delivers a formal introductory speech. Then Arafat speaks, emphasizing issues he believes will move a Frenchman's heart : the sufferings endured last year ; the mutilation of the Bethlehem Virgin : the use of depleted uranium munitions during the Jenin siege ; the current distress in the Gaza strip resulting from the bombings and demolition of buildings. He lingers on the Wall of Apartheid. No mention of the Geneva Understandings. Finally, he shows the Lorraine cross, a gift from General de Gaulle, which he wears around his neck. I'm told it is a ritual he performs every time he welcomes guests from France. The reception concludes with no less a ritual – a photo session. Arafat poses in the centre for a group photo and individually with each of his guests. The official photographer shoots incessantly. The on-duty cameraman films the entire scene ; it will be broadcast later this evening on the government channel.

Conversation in the evening with a Marxist activist from Hebron. He confirms many things heard in the past month. The Palestine resistance has been so thoroughly decapitated, so fractured, that it has fallen into the hands of tiny cells and largely uncontrollable individuals. Arafat will not take the risk of reigning in these extremist elements, which are behind many of the attacks, until Israel shows signs of implementing the " road map " or at least of partially drawing back its troops and settlers. " Why give the

Israelis such a gift ? " " Why should we be their policeman ? " " Why ignite a civil war in Palestine ? " The option of engaging these violent groups politically rather than crushing them militarily does not belong to the ethos of the situation. In nearly everyone's opinion, Oslo was an unmitigated calamity. For Palestinians material circumstances have never been worse in terms of unemployment, restrictions on movements, economic asphyxiation, expropriation of farm lands. Not to mention targeted assassinations, bombings, demolitions of Palestinian houses. The creation of a Palestinian state has never seemed more remote, in such flagrant contradiction with the reality of Israeli military domination. Every one seems resigned to life under a cycle of provocation-attack-reprisal. Everyone suspects Sharon of wanting to provoke Palestinians into a general uprising, which would create the pretext for mass repression and deportation beyond the borders of the West Bank. " Transfer " is the Israeli term for deportation. Is there a pilot in the Palestinian airplane ? Most people think not and are content to hang on, endure – until the enemy collapses under the weight of its contradictions. A depressing evening.

Interview with Refaat Sabbah, director of the " Teacher Creativity Centre " (TCC). On the door of his office, the portrait of Nelson Mandela. " Violence must not be allowed to become a value in our society. We formed our group to offer other forms of resistance. " Tall, affable, no beard, no moustache, he wears a simple white shirt and exudes a calm that is rare in Ramallah. His modesty is striking too. This thirty-nine-year-old former teacher of Arabic and director of the centre still makes the coffee for his guests himself. He receives me in a simple open office where members of the staff show up at any time.

Located on an upper floor of a downtown high-rise, the office looks out onto a vast horizon of rocky plains and olive groves. The front door still shows evidence of the Israeli army visit in 2002 during Operation Rampart (called here " the invasion ") : a big clump of solder where the lock was. Refaat recalls, " They simply blew away the lock with their Uzis, shot out all the windows, terrorized the employees and threw all the files on the floor. " Relatively minor damage in comparison with most public buildings.

Founded in 1995, the association's activity is civics education for the Palestinian education system, parents of pupils and municipalities. Its mission is to imagine new ways of promoting civic values. Refaat Sabbah has the stuff of a true educational pioneer. " During the first Intifada I realised that our society had become too tolerant of violence. This was evident in pupil-teacher relations at school. The struggle for national liberation appeared to justify all violations of human rights : women's rights, children's rights and the abolition of individual rights in general. I began by looking for solutions in my classroom and in school. Everybody thought I was mad. Then, gradually, we formed a small group and managed to find funds to launch TCC. "

Today, eight years later, TCC has fourteen permanent staff members and hundreds of volunteers. The association's results are truly amazing. It trains the trainers who reach out to over thirty thousand teachers (out of a total of forty-four thousand) in the West Bank and Gaza. Training sessions practice human rights in classroom management and school administration – at odds with classical civics teaching which is satisfied with a mere list of rights and duties. TCC programmes are supported by the Palestinian Ministry of Education and have received financing from the United Kingdom. Other activities are funded by the Ford Foundation, the European Union, the European Foundation for Human Rights and a raft of Canadian NGOs.

Refaat Sabbah is convinced that values are transmitted by example. Whether it is respect for others or respect for the law, children will only assimilate these principles if they see them in action at school. " Our educational system is dictatorial. Our teachers think their role is to transmit facts. They repeat them again and again and demand that the pupils learn them by heart. Teachers are as bored as their pupils ; everybody wants to leave school. But we would like them all to love school. The reason why TTC is successful is our belief that freedom lies at the core of learning. There is no creativity without democracy, without the development of a critical mind. If school only succeeds in suffocating the individual, creating constraints, nothing of value will ever come of it, especially not for children, who live under brutish circumstances. "

As far as Refaat is concerned, education and politics are interwoven. " Israeli society makes better use of democracy and transparency than we do. This gives them an advantage in the conflict with us. Our cause will triumph only if we succeed in assimilating human rights, if we learn to respect others : women, children and the weaker ones ; in short, only if our community learns to accept that everyone contributes equally to the development of the country. Victory won in the absence of democracy will inevitably result in dictatorship, as can be seen among our Arab neighbours. " TTC has taken this message to Israel, where it established ties with teachers' unions, until the year 2000 anyway.

The Palestinian Ministry of Education provided TTC with financial support to publish nine thousand copies of a manual for human rights defenders. The manual presents one hundred innovative activities – many very entertaining – to learn how to fight racism, sexism, intolerance and contempt for the law.

Refaat's immediate aim is to ensure that children stay off the path of violence. " Young boys run to the checkpoints and throw stones at soldiers and settlers. We tell parents to keep their children away from this until they are eighteen. We emphasise the right of each child to live and protect his own life. Recently we held a conference in Jenin on this topic. We went there fearing a very negative response to our non-violent message. (Jenin suffered heavy destruction in April 2002.) Exactly the opposite happened. The municipal authorities and political parties supported us actively. We held eighty-five workshops dealing with alternative forms of involvement in the resistance. Each workshop had around fifty parents. "

Another positive experience was a summer camp in 2003 for some one hundred twenty children aged eight to thirteen. " When the camp opened the children were detached, frightened, aggressive. They drew flowers which dripped blood ; in fact, blood figured in practically every single drawing. Little by little we managed to bring about changes in their behaviour and in their drawings, primarily by playing games. We made posters showing Palestinian children with other children : with Chinese, Africans, even Jews. It is important that they learn to see beyond Palestine, beyond the Arab world. We try to teach them to see the whole of humanity. The camp ended with a show that the children imagined entirely themselves. They staged it for their parents and the residents of Jenin. " The following month the same camp was run in Ramallah with one hundred forty-six children.

As director of TTC Refaat Sabbah says he no longer has time to teach ; he misses the classroom very much. He applies his educational principles at home with his two children. " I want my daughters to be clean inside. If I hear them say something against Jews, I don't let them get away with it. I remind them that Gayle, the wife of one of our best friends, is Jewish. And since they adore her, well you can imagine… " It's three o'clock and time for Refaat to pick up his children from school.

The next day. I am greeted by Reema Ajrami, a young female TCC staff member. Wearing a headscarf she surprises me with her liveliness, her perfect English and, above all, her firm democratic convictions. I stupidly thought a headscarf symbolised commitment to political Islam ; but what a mistake : Reema is uncompromising in her non-violent stance and denounces the Palestinian Authority for its weak policy on Hamas and its double talk. Obviously I still have much to learn here, which is fine. The day I think I know enough, it will be time to leave.

More memorable encounters this week.

Dinner with the sociologist Sari Hanafi ; he is an excellent cook. With May Jayyusi, a philosopher and director of the Palestinian Centre for the Study of

Democracy. We discuss the condition of the refugees. As they see it, my father, who fled Germany in 1933, was a refugee. I try to explain that the notion really doesn't apply either to him or to the other members of my family who went into exile. I doubt, in fact, that a Jew would consider himself a refugee. This is difficult for Palestinians to grasp. In order to consider oneself a refugee, you need to have a homeland, or at least a land where you belong and have ties, where perhaps you dream of returning one day. None of that in my family narrative. It's satisfying to air our points of view.

Another fruitful encounter : my neighbours invite me to a party where I meet Bachar, a young software engineer. We sit on the warm terrace among the flowers and talk into the night. He tells me about his friend Ronny, a Jew who lives in Tel Aviv. For two years they shared a room in an American university dormitory. Their families trembled in fright the whole time. These two kids from the Middle East shared nothing in common with their American counterparts. Though they haven't seen each other for two years, they stay in touch over the phone. Bashar, tall and handsome, wearing black jeans, hair cut like a rock star, is a sensitive, sentimental young man, who still hurts from his recent break-up with a Christian girl. " My mother is certainly not a devout Muslim, yet she rejected our relationship outright. " Bachar is trying to put together a rock band in Ramallah. He makes his own musical instruments from scrap materials that he finds in dumpsites. On his youth in refugee camps in Beirut : " The bodies were left in the street for days ; we played with the dead and took their watches. Human life was worthless. People killed for nothing –

for a wrong look. We lived with my parents and brother a hundred metres from the Chatila refugee camp. We were lucky, we left one week before the massacre. But honestly, there was so much more freedom in Beirut – no comparison with Ramallah. "

31 October – 7 November

My chronicle has a ring of scepticism and despair. I am resolved to put things in a more positive light, yet daily events frustrate my intention.

Construction. Ramallah is alive with building sites. The construction boom began after the Oslo Accords, particularly in Zone A (sixteen percent of the West Bank) under Palestinian Authority control. Souad Amiry, an architect, explains that the boom is due to demographic pressures and the fact that between 1967 and 1995 the Israeli administration refused to issue building permits, even for additions to an existing house or farm. True, every one regrets the tenfold increase in real-estate values in the city centre. True, cultured people fear the beautiful Ottoman-period villas will be sold to property developers, who will tear them down. True, there are more and more ten storey buildings, where once only one and two storey houses were common. But, hallelujah, let's be positive : more and more Palestinian capital is being invested here, a sign of confidence in the future of Palestine.

Road works. But of course the roads are destroyed every time Israeli tanks drive through the city, finding the streets too narrow. In Zone A – the only zone where the Palestinian Authority is allowed to decide works independently without risking an Israeli veto – the damage is repaired after each passage of the tanks. Funds from the European Union and the United States of America sustain the road maintenance vocation of many Palestinians.

Social standing. The flower shop employee in my street is a business school graduate. Down the same street the food store manager – he also works as volunteer manager of the cultural centre – is a law graduate. The nephew of my neighbour runs a falafel shop and has three employees ; he's a graduate of a hotel management school in the United States. My neighbour's cleaning woman has almost completed her Master's degree in English. But of course these highly-educated individuals feel frustration at not being able to use their knowledge and skills, a consequence of economic asphyxiation. I am more fortunate. I find an employee in the local travel agency who can spend half an hour discussing last night's performance at the theatre.

Games. There are dozens of Internet cafés in Ramallah, rather inexpensive : an hour for less than four shekels (80 cents). The clientele is primarily male, though some female students, usually wearing headscarves, come in for their email. Young children swarm in after school. They play video games, especially Formula 1 motor races. Seated in front of their screens teenagers and young adults shoot at anything that moves. Bang, bang. Like in real life.

Communications. Cell phones and satellite dishes, devices that leapfrog checkpoints and security fences, proliferate. The results are positive. I hear that Al-Jazeera's news reporting is so professional that local television coverage is very favourably influenced (the West Bank has some thirty network stations). In my romantic dreams I fantasize that cell phones expedite secret love affairs. I tell myself that thanks to satellite dishes television viewers can now watch something besides pilgrims circling the Kaaba in Mecca (granted this can be fascinating for insomniacs).

Food. Roads linking Ramallah to villages in the countryside can be closed for weeks on end. But of course the city takes the necessary precautions. The gardens have fruit trees. Sheep graze within two hundred metres of the Muqataa (or what remains of it). The ground floor of a four-storey residential building doubles as an urban chicken coop. Ramallah residents bring the countryside to the city in novel ways.

Delicious smells. On the patriotic principle that Israeli products must not be consumed unless absolutely unavoidable, pre-ground coffee can no longer be found in Ramallah. The happy result : every grocery store now smells of ground freshly coffee. The rich smell of freshly ground coffee wafts through the store and spills into the streets, even after curfew.

Still life. A lorry load of bananas arrives from the plantations near Jericho. But of course these small delicious bananas had to overcome one hundred administrative hurdles, travel two or three times more kilometres than necessary, and undergo at least five military inspections. But I find a certain charm in a banana cargo.

Marital bliss. Some stores display sexy lingerie in their window. Here a black-striped vermilion combination laced up in the front with gold fringes at the waist. There purple and pink G-string panties sequined in silver. Piously covered shoppers, head-to-toe in dark mono-coloured fabric, jostle inside and touch the lingerie, commenting on design. In contrast with other monotheistic religions Islam does not forbid the pleasures of sex – in the context of marriage, of course. I imagine the belly dance these pious women will perform for their husbands this evening.

Driving. But of course Palestinians ignore road signs and traffic lights, even when they do function. Because they drive on broken-up roads, bypassing countless obstacles and following tortuous itineraries, their driving skills are second to none on the planet.

Well-being. But of course the muezzin's call to prayer, amplified by the mosque's blaring sound system, wakes up the entire neighbourhood (largely Christian) at four a.m. every morning. But, God be praised, people of all beliefs are rescued from idleness and can enjoy the first rays of sunshine.

Security. My neighbours have uncanny powers of observation. Far better than any electronic security camera, they notice the slightest out-of-the-ordinary movement. The city's exits are now completely sealed and car theft has become quite ill-advised. The Palestinian Authority's secret services (and the Israelis, of course) control all firearms ; gangsters can hardly make a living anymore. Only domestic violence (rapes, beatings, honour killings) manages to remain at

" reasonable " levels, helped by curfews and overpopulation. Urban delinquency and petty crime have fallen so low I often forget to close my door.

In fact, my door was open when my neighbour Georgette dropped by and invited me to her flat for coffee. Here is Georgette Khoury's story.

" We lived in Ramleh, near what is now the Ben Gurion International airport in Lod. Our grandparents owned fields there. My parents were first cousins. Father had a variety of professions ; technician, mechanic, car battery repairman and school teacher. In 1948, like all men under fifty, he was arrested. He spent three years in prison until 1951. He died in 1955. My uncles – my father's brother and my mother's three brothers – and the eldest of my cousins were also imprisoned.

" We fled Ramleh when I was one month old. My brother was one, my sister two. Mother told me our story. She took refuge with her three children – me in her arms – in the nearby convent. She had only found time to grab our birth certificates and a few pieces of embroidered linen from her wedding trousseau. She watched from a convent window as the Jews ransacked our house and confiscated our belongings.

Then the Jews forced all the village women and children onto buses. The old people were told to stay behind. My grandfather, who was slightly deaf, did not hear the order and was shot in the knee. Pandemonium broke out. One woman – she was already on the bus – suddenly realised that the pillow she cradled in her arms was not her infant. She cried and screamed in despair. Later the same day, the buses stopped and everyone got off to sit under some trees for shade and rest (it was very hot). When everyone boarded the buses and the journey resumed, my mother realized she had left my sister Angela behind. My seven aunts (my father's three sisters and my mother's four) screamed and shouted until the driver turned around and drove back to the rest spot. Angela was still sitting there playing where we had left her. Had the driver not turned around the eight women would have murdered him on the spot.

" We were ordered off the bus and told to continue on foot. There was no water. Some women drank their own urine. The children were badly sunburnt.

" We ended up in the village of Bir Zeit with my aunts and cousins. We all lived in one room. The only light was a kerosene lamp, which we turned on for an hour in the evening before going to bed.

" When Father was released from prison, my parents hung a curtain through the middle of the room, a partition of sorts. He had suffered greatly in prison ; prisoners were not issued clothes, so they wore sacks to cover themselves. When they were served salted fish, they were given no water.

" Like other families, who lost their lands and homes in 1948, we were given refugee status. Our card gave us access to the schools and dispensaries managed by the UNRWA. We never lived in the camps. Few Christian families did. We only went there for free medical care.

" We lived in the West Bank under Jordanian jurisdiction until 1967. The Jordanians treated us properly, but the ceasefire agreement with the Israelis made it impossible for us to cross the border. Separated families had to communicate by radio. At

Christmas, Christian residents, who lived on the other side, received a three-day pass to visit their families. They travelled via Jerusalem through Mandelbaum Gate. In 1955 the nuns from the convent in Ramleh visited us. They brought my mother's linen trousseau. That is all we were able to rescue from our ancestral home. By chance, one day we found a wedding picture of my parents at my cousin's home in Cairo ; we copied it and distributed it to all the family members. Nothing else remains. Our land was called Thahabieh, literally " golden field ". When we saw it again after 1967 it had been transformed into a military airstrip.

" My mother raised her five children by herself, taking in sewing at home to earn a living. She worked for a charity and for the university. We helped as much as we could.

" I was sitting my high school final exams in Bir Zeit when the second Arab-Israeli war broke out. I had only two more papers to write when we heard the news on our transistor radio. Somebody offered to take me to the shelter, but I went to Ramallah instead, to an aunt who had a house near the main post office. When we heard that the baker still had some bread, we crawled to the bakery. Along the way four planes dropped their bombs ; they fell close to the girls' school. My mother heard the news and was certain we had been killed.

" Many people left Ramallah and Bir Zeit after that ; they did not want to live under Israeli authority, so they fled to Amman. But my mother refused another exodus and the additional risk of family separation. We stayed in Ramallah and won't move any further, no matter what happens. We won't leave this place. "

Georgette Khoury lives in a spacious flat that opens onto a garden, a short distance from the city centre. In a northerly direction hills stretch as far as the eye can see. Towards the east, I glimpse the Muqataa in ruins and several recently built residences. Vine runs along an arbour where Georgette has invited me to take a seat ; we chat over coffee and homemade apple spice cake. A polychrome stone virgin decorates a fountain. In her woollens (" twin sets " my mother called them) and tight trousers, there's something in Georgette's look that suggests the old British Empire ; the way she holds herself ; her figure, shaped by long athletic walks ; her uncomplicated, auburn coloured hair. She speaks fluent English with authentic concern for the proper word. There are framed pictures of her five children wearing graduation robes in her living room. End tables display wedding pictures, pictures of infants in prams, photos of family reunions. Doilies decorate the English fireplace ; plastic logs glow in electric fire light. Here and there faded pictures of religious figures.

Her grandchildren visit her every day after school for a snack. The garden is her husband's work, she says. The central flower bed, laid out around an ancient palm tree, features well-trimmed rose bushes. Lavender bushes, jasmine shrubs and bougainvilleas flower on the periphery.

Georgette's husband enjoys a rare and special privilege in Palestine : he earns a decent retirement income. For forty years he worked for the Jerusalem-Ramallah District Electricity Company founded by the British in the 1920s. In 1948 it came under Jordanian control and in 1967 the Israelis took it over.

84

Georgette's husband has never forgiven the Israelis for shutting down the Ramallah generators. The British brought the machinery by boat from Europe ; the Israelis left it to rust. Since then, West Bank Palestinians depend on electricity produced in Israel. Of course, the settlers obtain their daily supply without much difficulty.

Israel is plunging Palestine intentionally into underdevelopment. Georgette gives an example : her son-in-law's small business. " He manufactures metal and plastic objects : hangars, furniture accessories, etc. The raw materials came from Nablus. When the supply of raw materials was cut off, he had to terminate his three workers. Now he works the small factory with one of his brothers, who was also put out of work. " I have heard many stories about businesses forced to shut down due to travel restrictions. Jalal Khader, a business lawyer, told me about a client, a Ramallah cheese manufacturer, whose payroll fell from seventy to seventeen employees last year. He is still asking for financial compensation for milk product shipments that were blocked at checkpoints and left to spoil in the hot sun.

Wednesday. This morning Georgette visits the Amari refugee camp. From time to time she goes to the camp's handicapped youth centre for a neck and shoulder massage. She invites me to come along. The camp is just south of Ramallah on the road to Jerusalem. By and large it has been absorbed into the town, though it is still recognisable by its narrow streets and pre-cast concrete and parpen facades. There is not a tree or garden in sight. Few streets are paved. The camp's population density is higher than in Ramallah itself : officially seven thousand eight hundred people live within its tiny perimeter. The youth ratio is also extremely high : three thousand pupils attend UNRWA schools. Unemployment is chronic : seventy percent of the camp's household heads are out of work.

Dozens of school girls suddenly appear in the streets. They are in uniform and carry their school things in rucksacks. The younger ones wear a long blue-striped blouse worn over their trousers, usually jeans ; the high school-age girls wear a green blouse and headscarf, almost without exception. A twelve-year-old with rucksack greets us with a smile. I ask light-heartedly, " Why aren't you wearing a school uniform ? " – " I don't have to ; I have an exemption ", and shows off her Islamist style long black coat. Ten metres away an older man applies a coat of blue paint to his house. " He's my grandfather. He invites you for a soft drink at my uncle's shop, over there. "

At the corner of the main street, in the middle of the camp, five workers bustle around the building site of a new house. They are readying to pour concrete. Georgette remarks soberly, " The army demolished the previous house. Its owner is in prison. "

The local centre for handicapped youth is a modest facility that survives on charitable donations. It employs ten people, mostly women. A suite of tiny rooms on the ground floor are organized around a small courtyard. Each room provides a service : there is a room for physical exercise and massages, another for hair care and beauty therapies, another for educational games. In one of the classrooms a young female instructor reads a story to three mentally handicapped adolescents. Arafat's picture hangs on the wall to the left of the blackboard. The teacher invites one of the less handicapped children, Refaat, to recite the days of the week and months of the year in English. He succeeds with maestro ; everyone applauds. In the kitchen two chubby women prepare meals for the poor and the ill ; they are exempted from fasting during Ramadan.

The camp's health dispensary, managed by UNRWA, has much better funding and numerous people assemble here. By mid-morning at least one hundred people (mostly women) crowd the waiting room. A throng of women with small infants in their arms wait outside the infant care facility. One beautiful young woman presents her triplets to my camera : a girl and two boys, each lying in its own basket, dressed in a different colour ; they have come for vaccinations. Women – some wearing veils, some burkas, others with headscarves of every conceivable colour – sit on benches and stools, breastfeeding their infants. Despite the crush in the waiting room, the medical staff – only women, no head covering – remain polite and courteous.

UNRWA is often forced to make cuts in its basic services to the poorer segments of the Palestinian population (UNRAW's budget is voted by the United Nations). Other humanitarian organisations (charities and NGOs) try to take up the slack, especially in the refugee camps. Without their assistance Palestinian society would collapse. But now even the role of the NGOs is under challenge. Some argue that it is humiliating for the poor to depend on humanitarian aid ; that it is profoundly humiliating for the nation as a whole to depend on international assistance for its survival, particularly when home-grown talent clearly exists. The large financial donations from governmental and non-governmental sources – based in Europe, North America and the Emirates – raise serious political questions. The aid issue must be broached tactfully. In view of the international assistance it receives, Palestine survives on a lifeline. Why doesn't Israel bear the costs of education, health care and social assistance in the territories it has been administering since 1967 ? By alleviating the suffering of the Palestinian people and providing for their social welfare, hasn't the international community merely helped Israel shirk the cost of occupation ? (These questions come from a French senior civil servant working in Ramallah, who wishes to remain anonymous). Is the aid money always well spent ? In the end, don't the higher salaries paid by the international aid organisations (up to three times higher than those paid by the Palestinian Authority) drain away the best talent that the public service so badly needs ? Isn't a large portion of aid money channelled into reports (some say up to eighty percent) and never into action programmes ? Doesn't the aid money lead to corruption ? Is it right to allow the World Bank, UNICEF and this or that Swedish or Swiss foundation decide what the priorities of Palestinians should be or what the best means of achieving them are ? (These questions are from Hael al-Fahoum, an economist and PLO cadre.)

Then there are those who defend the NGOs as indispensable political counterweights. Rita Giacaman, for example, a national health consultant and director of the Master's in Public Health at Bir Zeit University, believes that certain needs of the population would never be met if it was not for the NGOs. She adds that they also provide a valuable public forum for democratic debate that, in the current political circumstances, it would be unfortunate to deny oneself.

But free and public debate is slowly ebbing away. Since 9/11 American NGOs are demanding that not one dollar of aid money be allowed into the coffers of terrorist henchmen. The NGOs have a long black list of terrorist organisations. Adila Laidi, director of the Khalil Sakakini Cultural Centre, must carefully vet the artists, writers and poets that she invites, with financial assistance from the Ford Foundation, in order to guarantee that they have no ties with the black-listed organisations. " But it's impossible ! There is not a single poet or artist that hasn't signed a petition demanding the liberation of some individual accused of terrorism ! And, besides, it is not our role to conduct police enquiries. "

Occupation generates many paradoxes. It creates high levels of poverty, unemployment, insecurity, injustice and humiliation. Yet paradoxically, thanks to the international aid, the levels of education, life expectancy and democratic aspiration continue to rise.

Saturday and Sunday. Demonstration days. I travel to Tel Aviv to meet friends. I haven't come here for six weeks. Crossing from one side to the other is always a shock. I stroll along the beach lined with luxury hotels facing the waterfront. The restaurant terraces in the old harbour district are already crowded at the beginning of the afternoon. The sun is still warm. Female cleavages, designer sunglasses, cool draft beer, starry-eyed couples in love, cute dogs on leashes, a gentle sea breeze, the scent of sea spray, the sound of waves, the long wooden walkway, an unending horizon stretching towards the West. In the evening I am invited to a private viewing at an art gallery and dinner in an Italian restaurant. I dare not narrate the events of this weekend when I return to Ramallah.

Fewer than five hundred people gather in front of the Israeli Film Institute in Tel Aviv. The event commemorates the fall of the Berlin Wall, but above all it protests the building of the new Wall, the " security fence " – four hundred seventy-five kilometres for the main structure, one hundred sixty-nine kilometres for the secondary fences. According to the latest " reliable " opinion poll (conducted by the University of Tel Aviv's Centre for Peace Research), only sixteen percent of Israelis are convinced that the physical barrier cannot prevent or eliminate terrorist attacks. Some nineteen percent are concerned that its path does not follow the 1967 Green Line*. The remaining seventy-three percent are not only in favour of the fences, they support the ground plan desired by the Israeli Government and the army.

Because the word " wall " is a misnomer – less than five percent of the total length is made of concrete slabs – and the word " fence " is clearly an understatement, from now on I will refer to it as the " Iron Curtain ". I must add that this multi-layered system runs along some really impressive " curtain rods " featuring electronic intrusion detection systems and advanced video surveillance equipment.

On the small square in front of the Film Institute the twenty organisations responsible for hosting the event have attracted their usual supporters, but not many others. While representatives of the various

---

* the pre-1967 border.

organisations take turns at the microphone, activists sell t-shirts that say in Hebrew, Arabic and English " War is not my language ". Old friends catch up on the latest news, while the many dogs frolic on leashes. Everyone agrees the event is a success (there have been worse turnouts).

Sunday afternoon. Back in Ramallah. On Al-Manara Square a much larger crowd gathers, perhaps a thousand demonstrators listening attentively to PLO speakers. They eloquently denounce Israel's " Apartheid Wall " and the latest woes inflicted on the Palestinian people (another five combatants killed this weekend, including a ten-year-old child). Lots of red flags are waved ; not many Palestinian ones. The crowd chants slogans similar to the ones I heard yesterday ; there is also a banner with a Star of David and a Nazi Swastika connected with the equal sign, something I have never seen in Tel Aviv.

In the papers this week I read two pieces of good news. In the Jerusalem Post I learn that the army is demanding additional credits to build more prisons. (The army was unable to conduct further arrests this week because there was no place to hold the additional prisoners.)

Also this week Colin Powell lends his support to the Geneva Understandings, to the great displeasure of Sharon and his cabinet members, who are leading a campaign against Yossi Beilin and the other Israeli signatories (they are denounced as " traitors worthy of court martial "). However, the next day the American ambassador issues a corrective statement stressing that Powell " encourages " the plan rather than lending his " official support ".

It has been raining since Sunday. An icy-cold wind leaves a thick mix of sand and dust on windows. Mist clings to the hills. From my balcony, high above a small valley, I watch the rain clouds roll up the slopes. The guardian of the corner building is busy removing posters with a knife. He has nothing against the heroes and victims ; the rain just makes it easier to clean the facade. In the local market handcart pushers slosh about in the mud ; country women hold their skirts above their heavy clogs. I can't imagine how people circulate between villages, refugee camps and checkpoints in these conditions. As for the cold, even the most comfortable flats lack central heating here. I have switched on a small gas heater and huddle close to it for minimal warmth. My thoughts are not happy ones : racism and dehumanisation are just some of the words buzzing in my head.

Nothing is easier than the dehumanisation of the " other ". You don't even have to be racist ; it suffices to reduce the other to a problem.

When my father, a radiologist, reached the end of a work day, he would say : " I still have a gall-

bladder and a collapsed lung in the waiting room. "
His view was that people were a medical problem.
End of story.

The Israeli view is that Palestinians are a security
problem. It can be resolved with soldiers, spies,
engineers, lawyers, Apache helicopters, F-16 fighters,
tanks, tear gas, stun grenades, fragmentation
projectiles, barbed wire, concrete slabs, and video
surveillance cameras ; myriads of gadgets that make
James Bond's arsenal look like toys for boys.

Seen from the point of view of humanitarian
organisations, Palestinians are a health and an
education problem. Secondarily, these organisations
can tackle culture, welfare assistance, human rights
issues, the struggle against sexual discrimination. They
rely on experts and a few hundred million dollars to
deal with these problems.

There are other problems as well – IDs,
passports, travel permits, economic asphyxiation, land
and property despoliation, lawlessness, constant
trauma, endless suffering... But because these
problems affect virtually every Palestinian, it is not as
easy to put them in neat little categories.

In the negotiations between Israel and Palestine,
efforts have been made to sort problems so they can
be dealt with efficiently. Because the 1948 refugee
issue is so charged, it has been set aside for later
treatment. And because the occupation and settlement
of territories conquered in 1967 appears easier to
resolve, it is given priority status.

So, here is the deal that both sides have been
working on for the past fifteen years. Israel : I'll return
what I took from you in 1967 (well, not quite, I've
annexed territory around Jerusalem and redrawn the

borders a bit to include some settlements). You can create a principality (actually two separate territories linked by a corridor), because apparently you think this is important. Now, in exchange, you renounce all your territorial claims, and you guarantee my security by eliminating all actual and potential agitators. And just to be safe, I forbid you to ever possess weapons. As for the refugee problem, for as long as it has been rotting in the freezer, why don't we just forget about it ? Do we have a deal ?

The deal doesn't work for hundreds of reasons. One, because Israel's right wing has not given up on the annexation of " Judea and Samara " and is not ready to withdraw behind the pre-1967 borders. As for the Palestinians, they continue to choke on the refugee problem ; because they see no way to disconnect the national struggle from the refugees.

First, the refugee problem is a statistical fact. There are some eight million Palestinians, of which four million are classified by the United Nations (UNRWA) as refugees. (Refugee status is accorded to those persons, and their descendants, who lost their homes and means of livelihood as a result of the 1948 Arab-Israeli conflict.) A million and a half live in the West Bank and Gaza (forty-two percent live in refugee camps). The others live in neighbouring Arab countries. The worst-off are in Lebanon (four hundred thousand). In addition to these card-carrying refugees, there are the despoiled Arab Israeli citizens transferred from their villages to other localities, the 1967 refugees, the persons expropriated by the Jewish settlers, and the Palestinians who resettled in North America, Europe, Saudi Arabia and the Emirates.

The second reason is historical. Palestinians discovered their national identity in exile and in the despoliation of their land. Until the end of World War I they were Arab subjects of the Ottoman Empire. The colonial division of spoils caused the Palestinian population to fall into British hands, while Damascus and Beirut came under the control of the French. After the British made promises to the Jews (the Balfour Declaration), the colonized peoples of the former province began to realize they would have to fight for their homeland. However, politically and militarily ill-prepared to resist the colonial powers and the waves of Jews arriving from Europe (not to mention the effects of inter-Arab conflict), the Palestinians lost the struggle utterly and completely.

Palestinian national conscience was forged rather late. In his memoir, *Out of Place*, Edward Said notes that his parents did not have one (though, he insists, his aunt Nahiba did). A generation later, the architect Souad Amiry confirms this when he says, " In the 1970s Yasser Arafat shaped my awareness that I belonged to a community which could fight to recover its homeland one day. Arafat can be criticized for many things – and I certainly do not hesitate to point out his mistakes – but I have to give him credit for raising my awareness. " (Could Arafat be Palestine's Joan of Arc ?)

Routed from their lands and homes in 1948, then again in 1967 and almost continuously since 1973 by the settlers, Palestinians are now virtually stateless (my father would say heimatlos), unwanted in their own homeland (the Israeli extreme right calls them " insects ", " cockroaches "). They have forged their Palestinian identity – inseparable from their consciousness as refugees – in the roiling cauldron of active and passive resistance.

UN resolution 194 guarantees the right of return of refugees and their descendants. This is not to imply that a majority are planning to exercise their right of return and to take possession of their parents' and grandparents' lands. Nevertheless, the right of return is their best card in the negotiations. How can anyone feign surprise that they play it so doggedly ?

Frankly, the idea that peace is possible before the " refugee problem " is solved – that it can be shoved under the table or pushed into the background until later – was necessarily born in the minds of people accustomed to slicing up problems into tiny pieces.

Sunday evening Hanane Rifi invites me to eftar (the evening meal that breaks the day-time fast during Ramadan). During the conversation she remarks : " What we should negotiate are the conditions for renouncing our claims. Because our rights as refugees are recognised by international law but not the occupation, which is totally illegal. The end to the occupation is a preliminary, not the principal aim. We have entered negotiations in the worst possible position. " Thirty years old, a translator-interpreter, Hanane Rifi and her husband, a manager for an American NGO, live with their two young children in an elegant flat in a new residential part of Ramallah. Far removed from misery. Far removed from the refugee camps. Far removed from Islamism. This young woman, who has not seen her parents in Gaza for three years, uses the same trenchant, acid words that Edward Said wrote ten years ago in reference to the Palestinian leadership. And others in Palestinian circles.

It is hardly surprising then that the Geneva Understandings, which follow closely in the footsteps of Madrid, Oslo and Camp David, create so little excitement. Since the official propaganda campaign has not yet started, the only people talking about it are nauseated that the refugees' claims are once again being abandoned. The majority have other concerns ; for example, the concerns of everyday life. They have seen so many agreements trampled under foot in the past ; so many hopes betrayed. A document signed in Switzerland between two private parties is hardly likely to rouse passions. The Iraqi " Intifada ", as it is called here, will probably stir more enthusiasm. But most people couldn't care a fig that the Israeli Left appears to be regaining some of its lost strength.

The sign that things are moving in the right direction will be the closing of checkpoints, the dismantling of the settlements, the reopening of highways, the return of soldiers to their barracks. It is not the extremists who say this, people who seek the destruction of Israel or call for revenge against the Jews (people I have not had occasion to meet). It is the kind little old Christian and Muslim ladies that I run into every day in Ramallah, the most moderate and bourgeois town in Palestine. In fact, Ramallah is so moderate that residents mockingly say : " We should send our Al-Manara lions to Jenin and replace them with mice... " The four marble lions at the base of the fountain sit stony-faced and indifferent.

What the Israeli Left is offering in Geneva, in exchange for a Palestinian abandonment of the right of return (and Greater Jerusalem), is the Noble Sanctuary in Jerusalem. The sacrifice is hardly significant because Israel has never established effective control over the third holiest shrine in Islam. The purpose of Sharon's walkabout with hundreds of his henchmen in September 2000 was paradoxically to assert with force Israeli claims to the site.

In negotiation after negotiation (the preamble of the Geneva Understandings mention at least ten) Palestinians are offered a fool's bargain ; proof, if need be, that they are mere colonised natives in the eyes of Israelis. To paraphrase a certain Karl Marx, they are the free transactions of an unguarded fox in the closed chicken coop.

Ramallah is certainly not a mirror image of Palestine as a whole. I am told to travel to Gaza, Tulkarm, Jenin – and of course the camps in Lebanon – to see the real tragedy of Palestine. " Ramallah leaves you with the completely wrong impression. Seventy percent of Palestinians live below the poverty line. Every week the army kills in Gaza and Nablus. "

I fear this chronicle of my peaceful days in Ramallah will distort my reader's perception of things. If only I could spend a week in the Balata refugee camp in Nablus or the Jabaliya camp in Gaza...

Well, except that...except that I'm not all that courageous. As I sit and watch the rain pour down, I am about as keen to trek to the refugee camps as I am to hang myself. Nevertheless, over the past six weeks I have visited three camps : Aida (Bethlehem), Shu'fat (Jerusalem) and Amari (Ramallah). Gaza and Jenin are only open to accredited journalists, not to writers and freelancers like me. Like most people here, including the residents themselves (unless they have special travel permits), I stay in Ramallah.

Because I do not speak Arabic, my contacts with the Arab Street are limited. I move in middle class circles, randomly among Christians and Muslims, men and women, English speakers and French speakers. Some people take the initiative to drop in on me. My neighbour Mussa, thirty years old, came by recently for a cigarette (out of the question to smoke in his parents' house during Ramadan). He stayed for over an hour and we smoked more than one. There was no language, class or cultural barrier. Consequently, everything seems so much easier. Less dramatic, but also more tragic.

If things go wrong at a checkpoint, I am able to cloak myself in my righteous Western indignation and unleash an offended cry, " I'm calling my Embassy immediately ". It's easy. It's what I did last Sunday when a soldier confiscated my digital camera. (To recover it I had to 'erase the picture of a father, a mother and their children arguing heatedly with Israeli soldiers.) No Palestinian enjoys such moral comfort. Against arbitrariness he is entirely without legal protection. When the occupier enters the tranquil city of Ramallah, he affords himself every right against the resident : he can pull him out of bed at two in the morning, forbid him to go into the street, even into his garden, destroy his car or his computer, confiscate his phone or take the keys to his car, throw his food supplies out the window, urinate on his carpets or his bags of flour, throw him in jail for as long as he fancies. If a Palestinian dies at the hands of a soldier or a settler, his family is offered no compensation. The parents of a child, the " collateral " victim of a fighter pilot's bombing run, do not even receive an official apology. There is nothing extraordinary in this ; nothing that would interest a reporter ; nothing that would make the nightly news.

The Palestinian philosopher, who visited me on Monday, May Jayyusi, makes a reference to Giorgio Agamben's notion of " bare life ", existence reduced to its mere bodily dimension.

It is possible to experience such existence, stripped of human dignity, on a drive through the Arab suburbs of Jerusalem. These outlying districts are lacerated by motorways that Arab residents cannot reach, that they have to bypass to reach lesser quality roads that the city of Jerusalem refuses to maintain, though Arab residents also pay local taxes for municipal services. One such Arab suburb, Beit Anina, can only be reached by driving under the motorway through a drainage ditch. Sewers and human beings... Whether these places are called Bantustans or ghettos, what does it matter ?

Users of Israeli motorways (also called bypasses) are protected from the awful sight of their Arab neighbours by a system of concrete slab walls, often covered in colourful graffiti. The best way to oppress a victim is to simply blank him out.

In philosophical terms May Jayyusi is exploring the relationship that the Palestinian suicide bomber has with his own body. She is particularly curious to explore what this relationship says about the political subject. At present she is studying writings by Foucault, Agamben and a few others. " Irish and Basque nationalists place bombs in cars. Ask yourself how a person can wrap a bomb around his own body and carry out an act which is contrary to human instinct ? I am studying the depositions of several failed suicide bombers held in Israeli prisons. Sometimes they took their decision after a long period of reflection ; sometimes it was very spur-of-the moment. One suicide candidate declared that he was looking out the window of his house, where he had been stuck under curfew for weeks on end ; he saw a dog gambolling about, playing with the soldiers, wagging its tail, running here and there. Suddenly he realised that the dog enjoyed more freedom than he did. Then and there he decided to become a suicide bomber.

I express surprise. Why so much attention to the behaviour, psychology and personal motivation of suicide bombers ? Why no blame of Hamas and Jihad ? Shouldn't the leadership denounce suicide operations as morally reprehensible, as counterproductive to the Palestinian cause ? Politely and patiently, May Jayyusi takes up the argument again, from the beginning. " Your thinking is too Western. Of course these attacks are detrimental to our cause in the West, but it can't be argued that they are counterproductive. Their impact on Israeli society is severe ; they ruin tourism in Israel and undermine Israeli morale. All acts of resistance – whether violent or non-violent, individual or collective – raise the moral and material cost of occupation for the occupier. At the same time, Islamist parties use the action to spread their political influence and weaken the PLO's leadership. Then again such attacks, which antagonise the two populations, push towards a two-state solution, which Hamas until now has always opposed.

May has no room for sentiments or moralizing in her politics. Her own calling is to develop her thinking freely. This tiny woman, nestled in her jumpers and scarves, thick black hair hiding her forehead, speaks in a soft, almost shy voice. Her mind is the most open I have met since arriving in Palestine (I feel a kindred spirit). A diplomat's daughter, she spent her youth travelling in the West and in Arab countries. She studied philosophy in London, where she met her first husband, a Jew from Hungary (or a Hungarian of Jewish descent ?), also a philosopher, and much older than she. They lived a liberated life, travelling widely. Relations with her Muslim family broke down. Her second husband, the father of her two children, is an Israeli Arab (a " 1948 Palestinian " as they call them on this side). May still leads a free and vagabond life. She works in Ramallah (which she finds provincial) and lives in East Jerusalem (which she says is suffocating). Her children live far away in London and her husband makes his home in Jerusalem (where she feels very uncomfortable, except when she goes to the cinema). She has lived out of a suitcase for the past eighteen months – perhaps since birth. She loves Beirut, London and large cosmopolitan cities. " And Paris ? – Charming, but perhaps just a little too charming. " Palestinians are said to be the Jews of our times. May incarnates this beyond the shadow of a doubt.

A conversation with my neighbour, Mussa, brings me back down to earth. This handsome young man, a graduate of Nablus University and an employee in a local bank, is engaged to Leila, a business school graduate. The future husband, as per tradition, has purchased a flat with all the requisite household furnishings. The wedding will be celebrated next June. By chance I met his future wife last week ; she is a dance and cinema enthusiast and directs a folk art centre. Mussa and Leila share many ideas in common. " We have no intention whatsoever of raising our children in this chaos that has been our daily lot for the past fifteen years. I can't count the number of school days lost because of the curfews. Honestly, before the Intifada life was not so bad. Every Friday with my parents we went to the seaside near Netanya for a picnic. We bought the latest fashions ; our friends in Jordan envied us. Instead of an uprising we should have tried our hand at democracy. Over the long run we would have obtained our rights. The Palestinian leadership, which had lived in exile for years, chose a different strategy ; it led nowhere, except to disaster. Frankly, I'm simply waiting for Arafat's leadership to end so that his successor can come onto the stage. Living side-by-side with Israelis we have grown used to democracy. If the only hope for Palestine is to become like other Arab dictatorships, corrupt and inept, then I prefer to live in Greater Israel and win back my rights little by little. My brother, Majid, doesn't think like me. Otherwise he wouldn't work for the Palestinian Authority. But he knows my opinions. " If anyone has doubts, freedom of speech is alive and well in Palestine.

Seated in an armchair, nursing a whiskey and smoking a cigarette, Mussa turns to the topic of religion. " I'm not an observant Muslim. Leila, she's a non-believer. My parents go to the mosque, my mother in particular, but they leave me pretty much alone. Leila's parents are the same. Leila and I can see each other everyday ; we go out together in the evening. This is possible in Ramallah ; not in Nablus, there it's a completely different story. I really suffered there. We had no freedom of speech, no freedom of thought. I can remember at least four or five students in Nablus who became suicide bombers. "

Since this first visit, Mussa now comes by every day. He drops in for a cigarette, a drink, a chat, or to listen to some music, to eat a few peanuts, to help me repair something in the flat. As his excitement for married life grows, day-to-day life with his old parents is becoming oppressing.

" My father is a refugee from Haifa. My mother comes from Tulkarm. When I was a kid, I got into a lot of trouble with some friends here. I was fourteen and I got caught throwing stones. I spent a week in prison. My father paid a huge sum to bail me out. He was told he could get his money back if I behaved for a year. He kept me on a very tight leash and after a year they gave back his six thousand shekels. That really settled me down. I don't want anything to do with violence anywhere. Frankly, when I see these young twenty-year-olds, who know nothing but violence, I say to myself, they're lost, completely lost. "

Thursday evening in Tel Aviv there is a " Marathon for human rights " organised by the Palestine-Israel Journal of Politics, Economics and Culture. Sari Hanafi will be speaking. He invites me to come with him. We join a group of Palestinian intellectuals travelling to East Jerusalem by minibus. On the way I chat with the historian Nazmi Ju'beh, one of the negotiators of the Geneva Understandings (he has been involved in every negotiation).

It is dark when we arrive in Tel Aviv, its brightly lit skyscrapers, motorway flyovers and neon signs dazzling in the night. I can't believe we left Ramallah barely an hour ago. The event is a huge disappointment. After a three-word introduction in English – words of welcome from the Irish

Ambassador who hosts the evening at the Tzavta Theatre – the other speeches are delivered in Hebrew (five minutes each). Even the pilot, Chagai Tamir, representing a protest group, and the amiable rabbi Ya'acov Rosenberg, who represents " Rabbis for Human Rights ", speak in Hebrew. I am particularly disappointed ; I would have enjoyed hearing them. There is no simultaneous translation and no effort by the Israelis to speak English (though they all do, fluently). The Israeli flag is displayed on the podium ; a stand for the Palestinian flag remains empty (the organisers were counting on the Palestinian delegation to bring a flag). There are some two hundred Israeli militants in the auditorium and fifteen silent Palestinians. Sari Hanafi is boiling with anger. After a musical interlude, it will be his turn to speak. Yaffa Yarkoni, the singer, comes on stage for four patriotic songs. " Does everybody understand Hebrew ? " she calls out to the audience. She's the first person in over two hours to ask the question. A few scattered voices shout back " No ! " and she carries on gleefully with a few strains of a Israeli patriotic song from the Independence War (the "Palestinian nakba "). Humming and clapping along, the Israeli audience knows the repertoire by heart. A boy-scout atmosphere. By now Sari is livid, but he nevertheless applauds politely. At last it's his turn to take the microphone. As the good sociologist he is, he observes mordantly (in English with a slight Arabic and French accent) that the asymmetry between occupier and occupied is well represented this evening, especially in this auditorium where the Palestinian presence is token. There is sporadic applause from the audience. He then launches into his

106

prepared remarks and severely criticizes the Israeli and Palestinian human rights movements for their contradictory attitudes. At 22.30, as scheduled, the Palestinian contingent leaves the venue and climbs aboard its minibus, leaving the Israeli pacifists to their marathon (i.e. to their " solo " effort). A wasted evening, not one ounce of dialogue ; coming from the Palestine-Israel Journal it is shocking. On the return trip to Ramallah it is decided to send a firm collective statement of protest. No illusions as to its impact.

A few more things seen.

Woman in black. The minibus between Kalandia and Jerusalem stops at an intermediary checkpoint. A young soldier rolls open the back door. Everyone shows an ID, including a woman wearing a black head-to-foot burqa and gloves. With an infant in her arms she shows a green identity card (a West Bank Palestinian). The soldier hesitates a fraction of a second then growls, " OK. Have a nice day. "

Boys will be boys. I hear bursts of automatic gun fire in my street. To my knowledge there are no Israeli tanks in town at present. A hundred or so unarmed shebabs run in every direction, their faces fierce. (Shebabs are Palestinian youths – mid teens to early twenties – who fight against the Israelis.) Cars speed away, tires screeching. A young man waves a machine gun in the air. Bursts of gun fire continue. Groups of adolescents flee, converge again and re-form around an invisible enemy. The caretaker of a building and the owner of an Internet café watch from their doors. " It's just a fight between two kids. They probably called in their friends. The one with the gun probably belongs to some security organisation. People shoot into the air a lot here to create fear. But it's rare that anybody gets hurt ; if something serious happens, the brothers of the victim have to protect their honour and take revenge ; then things can get nasty.

National holiday. Flags are draped on the metal scaffold frame towering over Al-Manara Square. The Palestinian Authority has decreed November fifteenth Independence Day, a public holiday. (Sadly a few people find this funny.) Some morose-looking scouts march by beating their drums. Their elders string up a banner denouncing the " Apartheid Wall ". They quickly leave the square and make way for the militants of the Popular Struggle Front who shout far less pacifist slogans. Late in the afternoon Fatah militants march, demanding the liberation of Marwan Barghouti, Member of Parliament. The four lions sit stony-faced.

To round off the week here are a few news items picked from the press.

The headline of the Israeli daily Yediot Aharonot quote four former heads of Shin Beth, Israel's internal security agency, who declare : " We are headed for disaster " ; " Each day that goes by, we sink deeper into the bloody mire and the economic and international price we are paying for this is getting steeper. "

A sudden turn of events in Serbo-Bosnian relations : the Prime Minister of Serbia presents a formal apology for the sufferings caused the Bosnian people. Eight years after the end of the war the borders are re-opened and a cooperation agreement is signed.

That's it for the good news. Friday, thirty Italian carabinieri are killed in Iraq. Saturday, there are two attacks against synagogues in Istanbul.

I am stuck between two questions. 1. When will we reach the bottom of the abyss ? 2. Is there a bottom ?

Sunny days, ice cold nights, wild swings of temperature. The desert lies close to Ramallah. Here the sweltering humidity of the coastal regions is never to be felt.

The Palestinian coast has been twice lost. Jaffa and Haifa, the two major port cities, prospered under an urban, westernised, cosmopolitan and increasingly secular bourgeoisie, which earned its living from commerce. In the 1940s, it began to invest in small industry, frequently in association with Jewish entrepreneurs. Nablus, the largest West Bank city, was in the hands of a few wealthy land-owning families. Sally, who comes from Tunis, says, " Palestinians lost their lands but kept their rural mentality. " Souad, the academic from Beirut, puts the idea in more technical terms, " the loss of the coastal region resulted in a conservative retreat into the provincial hinterland. "

Everyone is making preparations for Eid. Families from the countryside on shopping sprees for the festivities, fill the markets and streets of the city centre. Peasant women wear long black embroidered robes. Men don a traditional, black and white checked keffiyeh. There is the usual blaring horns and impatient shouts of drivers in a snarl of yellow taxis and delivery vehicles. Grandmothers carry huge bundles gracefully on their heads. The shebab kindly lend a hand, helping them load up or unload in the jostle of the street. Vast quantities of food spill from the fruit and vegetable crates. Colours are teeming : the deep red of pomegranates, the vivid yellow of banana stems, the bright green of parsley, mint and sage. The haggling over crates of dappled aubergines, baby courgettes, persimmons, clementines and limes is intense. The heady scent of guava overpowers everything else. Tensions mount among the hawkers. An old peasant, crouched on his heels and looking exhausted, sells goat's cheese, which he offers with large, incredibly worn hands. In the crowd I am the only person who succumbs to observation. Progress is slow along the pavements overflowing with stalls ; sometimes Palestinian policemen drive away the hawkers. During Eid children receive all kinds of gifts : warm clothes, toys and money. A mother plunges her arms up to the elbow into a pile of pullovers, checks the size of one and presses it to the shoulders of her strapping son. Sheepishly the boy looks elsewhere, feigning disinterest as best he can. Shoes and lingerie come from Turkey ; blankets, trousers and bazaar articles from China ; appliances from Korea. But, in fact, all these imports are handled by Israeli wholesalers ; the goods are unloaded in Israel, then reloaded onto Israeli lorries and transported to Palestinian markets, tagged with labels in Hebrew. Realistic-looking, black plastic AK 47s and M16s are plentiful. A friend remarks, " Isn't it a dangerous present for a child? From a distance a soldier could mistake it for real. Or pretend he did... "

Most people, who fast, wake up at four a.m. and, after prayers, eat a full breakfast. It has to keep them going until sunset (which presently is at four thirty p.m.). After prayers and breakfast they are allowed to go back to bed, if they wish. I know people who interrupt the fast when they feel weak or forget to wake up. I know others who don't even bother to fast. Bachar, the computer engineer-cum-rocker, says " I used to fast when I was younger, but it was bad for my health : I felt weak, unable to do anything worthwhile. Anyway, I've lost my faith. " Others become impatient, like the owner of the juice bar on the square : " I haven't had a drop of alcohol this month. When Ramadan is over I'll get together with some friends for a few drinks. Everyone brings his own bottle of whiskey. " My neighbour, Mussa, for example, says : " Starting next Tuesday, I won't have to come to your flat to smoke. " But until then, the city will suddenly empty every afternoon at four. Eftar takes on a party atmosphere. High-end restaurants offer a feast spoiled by cheap music for sixty shekels (eleven euros) ; at the lower end of the scale one can eat for twelve shekels (two euros). Most people just have a meal at home with family or friends.

During the month of Ramadan those who pray do so with special fervour, particularly in the last few days before Eid. Mosques are never empty.

Last Friday, at about ten in the morning, a surging crowd of men and women pressed at the Kalandia checkpoint. Under the crush some people began to climb over and around the concrete blocks. On the verge of being overwhelmed, the guards started shouting and threatening the crowd with their automatic weapons. Unimpressed, the crowd didn't budge. The situation was on a knife's edge ; tragedy loomed. A passer-by told me, " It's the same every Friday, even worse during Ramadan. Everyone wants to pray at Al-Aqsa Mosque. It's not a religious obligation, but it's a tradition here. " Al-Aqsa is more than a Holy Place ; it's an emblem. One sees representations of its golden dome rising above the walls of the old city virtually everywhere : on prayer rugs, on posters honouring victims, in cafés, even in the background of official pictures of Arafat. If ever Palestine prints banknotes, they will surely bear the effigy of Al-Aqsa Mosque.

In Palestine it is difficult to separate Islam and national identity. Very few people recommend the exclusion of religion from public life. Most liberals compromise with Islam but oppose its most common misinterpretations. This is how George Khleifi, the filmmaker, explains it : " The Qur'an allows for the stoning of an adulterous woman on condition that four adult males actually witness the lover's penis penetrate the female sex. But since this condition is never met, by rights imams should not authorise lapidating. The same can be said of suicide operations : the Qur'an formally forbids the killing of civilians. No imam should ever condone such an act. " In fact, they rarely denounce the more obvious expressions of intolerance. A simple example : no one would ever call for a lowering of the decibel levels of the neighbourhood mosque's loudspeakers. " It would be impossible to raise the topic at a city council meeting ; it would simply be taboo ", says Mussa, my neighbour. But the same city council can authorise a

114

ban on alcohol in cafés and restaurants during Ramadan. And the Ramallah city council did so three years ago. Christian shopkeepers, and even some Muslims, are unhappy with the measure, so they continue to serve alcohol, albeit discreetly. At café X (I avoid identifying the establishment for fear of reprisal against the owner) wine and beer are served in large porcelain cups. But what happens when a young Muslim woman finds a note in her handbag, " headscarf or hell " ? " Nothing ", says Bachar, " it happened to my neighbour this week, a student at Bir Zeit. Most of the time the girl merely puts on a headscarf to avoid any further trouble. "

Then again, there are different kinds of headscarves. There is an abyss between the woman I see covered from head to toe in a heavy black button-down garment and the young bourgeois woman sitting next to her, wearing make up and jewellery, tight jeans, high heels and a colourful scarf held by a glittering clasp. At least the covered woman's face is visible. Some show only their eyes while others cover their hands and face completely. I know from experience that a scarf reveals nothing of a woman's thinking. To be thorough on this topic of head gear, let's not forget the " bearded " ones, who wear brown turbans or white caps, nor the men folk from the country, who wear checked keffiyeh, sometimes tied around their necks like a scarf.

Some in the leadership are capable of bold decisions. Safa Tamish recounts how, ten years ago, she received an invitation to deliver a series of lectures on sexual education at Bir Zeit University. She had only recently completed a degree in the field at New York University, the first Arab woman to do so. She was expecting twenty-five students for the first seminar when some four hundred showed up in the lecture hall and surrounding areas, most of them titillated onlookers, but also a large number of Islamist activists shouting slogans and distributing leaflets. The hullabaloo was colossal, but young Safa did not back down and the president of the university defended her, threatening to expel the troublemakers. The following seminars took place without further incident.

Such firmness on behalf of figures of authority is not common. Last October the Goethe Institute had scheduled a concert of contemporary music on the campus of Al-Quds University in Jerusalem, in association with the cultural affairs department. Johannes, the young trainee who currently shares my flat, was responsible for welcoming the musicians and helping them set up for the event. He still hasn't fully recovered from the emotion of the experience. " Before the concert could begin a throng of bearded fanatics swarmed onto the stage. They overturned all the amplifiers and stage equipment. We were just able to rescue the musical instruments and run to safety in the offices of the administration, where we were virtually held hostage for three hours until we could get free. " On that particular day Sari Nusseibeh, the president of the university, was not on campus (he was busy with the peace negotiations). Hamas considers music – Western or otherwise – pointless and ungodly ; it does not have a place on campus. The same evening the guest musicians gave a successful concert in another hall in East Jerusalem.

" Islam has never modernised because it has never been confronted with the kind of opposition the

116

Catholic Church has had to face since the Reformation ", explains the historian Nazmi Ju'beh. " The circles of power and influence remain unstructured and difficult to combat. Palestinian people have never really been religious, but in the past ten years Islamist militants have made in-roads. Actually, their ranks swell when prospects of a peace agreement wane and they shrink when hope is bright again. At the beginning of the 1990s Hamas represented may be five or six percent of public opinion. When a population despairs, it commits itself into the hands of God. It's also important to consider the changes in the region since the Islamic revolution in Iran and the collapse of the Soviet Union. " My friend Malika confirms this in her own way : " In periods of crisis urban women take to wearing scarves, which they remove as soon as things get better. " Islam is an essential safety valve for many and a political ideology for some. Secularism, as it is understood in France for example, has no place here in Palestine. Simple tolerance would be a splendid objective.

Some of May Jayyusi's thoughts in the area of politics and religion astonish me quite frankly. She hates the compromising attitude and colonial submissiveness that one calls, somewhat disdainfully here, " the spirit of Oslo ". " These people are negotiating without any mandate from the people. They are not even approaching the issues from the point of view of our rights, but from the point of view of what the Israelis might be willing to concede. They are corrupt politicians, who are prepared to kneel at the feet of the occupier merely to retain their tiny parcels of power. They give up the struggle before they obtain anything at all. At least the Islamist militants fight without compromising ; they couldn't care less what the West thinks about them. They've broken entirely with the colonial mindset. "

This late evening talk leaves me ill at ease. " May, how can you say such things ? If the Islamist groups " free " Palestine, you'll be the first to leave the country. How is their thinking less colonial than others ? Wasn't political Islam systematically encouraged by the United States throughout the 80s ? " Because we are good friends May and I agree to continue our conversation sometime again in the future with fresher minds.

Many Palestinians have helped me understand something I have been reluctant to admit : the Islamist parties, who sometimes sit on the Palestinian National Council and sometimes don't, belong to normal political life here. They express a current of public opinion that has its political legitimacy. It is, in fact, no more or no less legitimate than any other, regardless of whether the West finds it unacceptable, at least for the moment. They occupy a place in Palestinian national politics that recalls the radical Jewish parties in Israeli political life. As for the divide between terrorists and non-terrorists, it makes very little sense for either side, as virtually every political leader in the region has been accused of terrorist activities at one time or another (and many continue to be involved in such activities). Take for example the countless Israeli streets with the names of Zionist leaders, who won their reputations in terrorism. Likewise the division between democratic and non-democratic parties is vain. " If democracy is what the United States is giving to Iraq or what Israel is forcing on us, then no thank you ", says Inam with bitter irony.

Mudar Kassis, director of the Law Institute at Bir Zeit University, gives me an appointment to discuss the Geneva Understandings. He lives in a modern villa in a residential suburb of Ramallah. Though it is already late, the phone rings constantly, and I have ample time to admire the furnishing, which is contemporary, elegant and functional. Professor Kassis' working days are decidedly long. His young wife and five-year-old child show their faces from time to time. Mudar Kassis develops his arguments with deliberation.

" Did you take part in the Geneva Understandings ? " I ask.

– Not at all. Please feel free to ask me any questions you like.

– What positive outcome can there possibly be ?

– As you know, it's an unofficial document, so probably the best outcome might be : 1. to give an idea of what the final agreement might look like ; 2. to provoke public debate on topics that are basically taboo in our two societies ; 3. to illustrate the absurdity of Sharon's central thesis that there is no negotiating partner on the other side. Then, at an even higher level, I can see positive outcomes for the democratic debate among Palestinians themselves. Since this is the first political text that has not been shaped by the PLO, people will feel freer than usual to discuss it. It is also the first time that Palestinians are invited to debate a text before it is signed and, indeed, that a text is even presented to both sides for popular approval.

– Concerning the text itself, in your view, is it a step forward ?

– Compared with the agreements before it, it's the first to refer specifically to resolution 194 (the refugees' right of return) and it's also the first to mention the need for compensation for losses caused by the settlements (thus, compensation not only for the refugees but for others as well). Another positive development is the principle that the new State should recover one hundred percent of all territories lost in 1967 (at least quantitatively, which means land swaps are possible). And the final point, in my view, is the full and unrestricted recognition of Palestine's sovereignty as a state. After careful reading these are the only positive outcomes I can find.

What about the negative ones ?

One. The equality of the parties is affirmed in the preamble, but it is not maintained in the remainder of the document. For example, the Palestinian state is obligated to disarm, but there is no equivalent obligation on Israel, not even in the field of nuclear weapons. Either disarmament is an individual choice, or it is an obligation for both parties. It is worrying that Israel remains free to augment its military strength. Given the tensions in the region today, Israel is of course not ready to disarm, but we should at least demand that it agrees to a negotiated settlement with its neighbours leading to mutual disarmament. For fifty years Israel has been the aggressor, yet it offers nothing in exchange for our agreement to relinquish weapons.

Two. There is no mention of the word " occupation " anywhere in the document. Yet Palestine must be decolonised. A peace agreement has to take into account the damage caused by the Israeli occupation : infrastructure underdevelopment ; curbs on health and education ; economic hurdles, etc. Anyway, Israel will not pay for the costs of colonisation, the European Union will. But Israel should at least assume its moral responsibility.

Three. The rights of refugees. The application of a right of return does not mean that one hundred percent will come back. This cannot be our position. Moreover, it would be paradoxical if the new sovereign Palestinian state were to make a citizenship claim for its own nationals in the neighbouring country ! But the rights of each individual must be recognised. It is the right of each person to decide whether " the return home " means back to the 1948 territories inside Israel or to the land inside the borders of the new Palestinian state. Haaretz published an article this week showing that, based on a sociological analysis of Palestinian refugees around the world, very few statistically speaking, plan to exercise a right of return. Hopefully this will reassure the Israelis. The right of return is a very private issue, which is only negotiable if there is a specific mandate from the persons concerned.

Moreover, on the matter of refugees, Israel should – at the very least – recognise its responsibility ; in other words it should recognise the full rights of the refugees. And both parties should agree to cooperate in regard to facilitating the return of refugees to the Palestinian state without prejudice for their right of return to Israel.

In exchange, Israel might ask that beneficiaries, exercising a right of return and deciding to live in Israel, would nonetheless have Palestinian citizenship and have a right to vote in Palestine. Thus, the right of return would not translate as an acquisition of Israeli citizenship.

Four. The international security force. Its status must be guaranteed by a UN Security Council decision. If Palestine is disarmed, this force will be our only protection. Israel must not be allowed to exert any means of pressure on it.

Five. Lands. The only justification for land exchanges should be to avoid that people are forced to move once again. But we should not consider the existence of symbolic places or the fait accompli of certain settlements.

Six. External borders. Israel is requesting thirty months for the withdrawal of its military forces and settlers from our borders with Egypt and Jordan. It should be the responsibility of the international security force, and not the Israeli army, to guarantee the transition phase. Why should the entire world trust Israel when Israel itself refuses to trust anyone ?

– What do you say to opponents of negotiations who argue that the current power balance does not favour a " just peace " ?

– The context is marked by some harsh realities : Israeli military domination, economic liberalism's global domination, and the United States's global domination. In this highly unfavourable context Palestinians could reject negotiations with Israel and demand the full application of international law and the rights of refugees. But the price to pay for this radicalism would be steep for the population. Is such a price reasonable ? There are people both inside and outside the camps, who are ready to make the sacrifice, who think there is nothing to lose, who believe that things can't possibly get any worse. There is, of course, a price to pay for negotiations. Today, we not only have a responsibility to convince our own people that peace is possible ; we have to convince the Israelis as well. We have to convince the Israelis since their own elite is not enough to say that there will never be a " Great Israel " nor a " Pure Israel ". If we are under pressure to make concessions today, it's also because of our own mistakes in the past : our rejection of the 1947 plan of division of Palestine, our refusal, until 1974, to recognise Israel's right to exist, not to mention our mishandling of Arab friendships.

– In other words, you support the peace process in the name of political realism ?

– Intellectuals have an obligation to maintain emotional detachment. After defeat, there's a price to be paid in this world, which, whatever one thinks, acknowledges might. We are already making a concession if we accept a political solution rather than a purely legal one. Fundamentally, I think we should move as quickly as possible to self-determination. It is the one condition that will enable us to make socio-economic progress : employment, income, education and health. Undeniably, on one level, socio-economic interests are in conflict with the national interest. I think we should take the first interests into consideration as a matter of priority. This is how the Europeans manage their own integration process. Each member state makes concessions of national interest in order to achieve real or supposed benefits for all. The time we have spent, since 1948, discussing the right of return, I would have frankly preferred a discussion of health, education and economic development. Just like you in Europe.

Realism demands we accept that there are only nine million Palestinians in the world. We are a tiny people and we need to set ourselves goals within our reach. "

Mudar Kassis tries to keep his feet on the ground ; not very easy when your country is without land. When the interview becomes personal, the renowned professor, who was born into a Christian family, trained in the Soviet Union and was a long-standing member of the communist party, calls himself a " radical Marxist " and a " militant atheist ".

Now he has some questions for me. When I tell him that my articles are sometimes published in a secular leftwing Jewish publication, he asks somewhat surprised, " How is it possible to be Jewish, secular and leftwing ? " – Some of us accept our heritage and try to make something out of it. Of course it means we must not clad our Jewishness in mere religion, even less in faith, as is common in France. " Our conversation reels us back into memories of our respective childhoods. Mudar Kassis recalls some of the Christian schools he attended (because they were the best in Palestine) and the prayers he was forced to recite every morning. In contrast I went to secular state schools in France. Jewishness was restricted to the sphere of my family and friends, closely associated with my grandparents, religious celebrations, a far-flung family living on several continents, political debates that animated dinner conversations and the many happy and unhappy memories that shaped who I am. As I get ready to leave, the little girl hugs her father's legs. " We won't celebrate Christmas, but I'll buy her a tree just the same. It's so important to her. "

The conversation brings me back to my earlier thoughts. If there are many ways of being Jewish, why wouldn't there be different ways of being Muslim, or at least to receive a Muslim heritage ? Aren't there " secular, progressive Muslims " who recognise Islam as part of their cultural identity, yet refuse to allow it to block the horizon ? I am inclined to compare Islam here to Catholicism in Poland ; isn't it the cement of national identity when confronted with too much adversity ? Like Polish priests, Islamic militants can make themselves highly useful in the area of social assistance and child care. I like to hope that, when national liberation has come about, it will be possible to bring the religious leaders back to reason and to their " rightful place ".

Crossing the Surda checkpoint recently I had a good fright. The checkpoint appeared unguarded when suddenly at very high speed an ambulance followed by two lorries and three taxis raced down the eight hundred metre stretch of paved no man's land separating the two roadblocks. Frantically sounding their horns, accelerating and braking recklessly, the vehicles forced their way through the pedestrian crowds and push carts, leaving everyone to scramble for safety – and their lives. When this happens, if the Israeli army arrives, pedestrians can find themselves in the line of fire. And last week it did happen to Filali, a French lawyer, on his way back from Bir Zeit.

Scenes like this happen everyday in Palestine. People will do anything to pass a checkpoint or avoid a ban. Taxis sometimes follow tracks through the hills ; they travel down passages so narrow that they risk overturning into ravines. The only thing drivers refuse to do is turn around ; they simply will not bend to the occupier. " It's a matter of honour ", says a French employee at the Consulate who has lived in Palestine for ten years. Palestinians use the word sumud, meaning resilience, resoluteness.

The newspaper headline reads, " Thousands of Palestinian militants in Gaza and the West Bank demonstrate against the Geneva Understandings. Hamas and Islamic Jihad label negotiators traitors, insisting on the sacred right of return and their refusal to lay down weapons. "

The Israeli newspaper Haaretz reports, " Two hundred thousand Palestinian Muslims pray at the Temple Mount on the last Friday of Ramadan " ; Temple Mount is the Israeli term for Al-Haram al-Sharif.

Let's conclude this chronicle with some good news.

In the newspaper (Haaretz again) I read : Friday, a tank driver refused his captain's orders to shoot a Palestinian caught placing a roadside bomb near a settlement in Gaza. The Palestinian managed to escape and a bomb squad defused the bomb. An enquiry has been opened.

At the beginning of the week Hélène, my new flat mate, arrived from Marseilles. Three of us now share the flat. This tiny freckled woman (French mother, Palestinian father and husband) always amazes me. Though she grew up among the Touaregs and her parents were penniless, she managed to overcome unbelievable hurdles and recently completed a doctorate in geography on the urbanisation of refugee camps in Palestine. Since Johannes is the son of a protestant minister and Hélène Muslim, we raise our glasses to the union of

126

the three great monotheistic religions living under one roof. Except that Hélène drinks tea, Johannes beer and I a glass of wine.

Monday, during the night, I return to my Penates in Ramallah after nearly a week's absence.

On this first of December the parallel Israeli-Palestinian diplomacy achieved official consecration in Geneva. At noon the same day, Israeli tanks completed large-scale manoeuvres in downtown Ramallah. I was not in Ramallah in the night of Sunday to Monday, when ninety Israeli tanks supported by helicopters surrounded two buildings suspected of harbouring two Hamas militants ; so I did not see the bodies of the two militants killed during the battle, nor the body pulled from the ruins of a neighbouring building the following day – allegedly the " big fish " the Israelis were pursuing – nor the body of a nine year old boy killed in a demonstration in the Al-Amari refugee camp the same day. Nor did I see the funeral procession, which formed the next morning and proceeded from the central mosque to the cemetery ; so I will limit my commentary to what I did see and hear myself.

Incidentally, many journalists leave the impression that they have been everywhere, seen everything. I make no such claim.

Monday evening. I arrive in Ramallah much later than planned. My flight was delayed two hours because of a strike at Tel Aviv airport by ground staff (strike action is rife in Israeli at present). Since the checkpoint on the main highway at Kalandia closes at nine pm, my driver – an Arab from Jerusalem related to my landlords in Ramallah – takes an alternate route. Instead of forty-five minutes, we allow two hours for the journey on dirt tracks through the hills, including many stops and perilous manoeuvres to allow traffic from the opposite direction to circulate. I cannot recommend strongly enough this scenic route. Five kilometres beyond the airport we turn left off the four-lane highway onto a secondary road, which we take through the plain for several more kilometres. We reach a small guardhouse manned by a single sleepy orderly, who examines the first page of my passport with a half-raised eyelid, then we enter the West Bank. It might be better to say, we climb to the West Bank, so rugged and steep is the landscape. The distance between the first Palestinian village and the airport is no more than fifteen kilometres. This coastal region, pre-1967 territory of Israel, is very narrow. My grandmother constantly worried that the Arabs would cut Eretz Israel in two, isolating the North from the South. Now seeing the territory first hand, I am able to understand her fears.

It is difficult to imagine a starker contrast. Hitchcock's political thriller, Torn Curtain, takes us from the familiar world of the West into the frightening world of the DDR, swarming with spies

130

and other creepy creatures. Light bulbs emit pallid light, central heating is defective, the plumbing leaks, doors creak. When one crosses from Tel Aviv airport to the Palestinian villages on the other side of the 1967 border, one tears a similar curtain in under fifteen minutes. With an important difference, as far as I am concerned : I breathe more freely on the Arab side.

This last remark certainly requires explanation. But I fear my reasons will sound laboured and confused. Let's keep it short. My driver walks on thin ice when he moves among Jews ; he avoids speaking Arabic, tries to make himself inconspicuous, despite a husky rugbyman's build. But on the other side of the Green Line, he greets the village people as he drives by ; he chats with the other drivers. As we speed along now at thirty miles an hour, he relaxes. I lower the window to breathe in the night air and smoke a cigarette. I love the journey. The scenes of village life are more exciting than the dull motorway rest areas of the western world we have left behind. Wrecked cars pile up along the road side. In the distance, we see only the green neon lights of minarets, up closer the pale neon lights of grocery shops still open at this late hour. Off to the side of the road the silhouette of a peasant woman struggling home under a heavy load emerges from the darkness. Shehabs in jeans and leather jackets chat late into the night at a food bar. I vow to travel this road again during the daytime.

Tuesday morning. A violent storm erupts. Thunder interrupts my sleep. Lightening. Heavy rain. My only loss, the modem of my portable computer. Looking for a solution I explore what Ramallah has to offer. Many young people here are highly skilled computer experts. They are polite and patient. They don't often have the opportunity to help a woman their mother's age. In the meantime I missed the funerals. I am told the crowds were huge.

Few people in Ramallah join political demonstrations. (I often hear, " What is the sense of demonstrating by the tens of thousands in the streets ? Nobody is going to listen anyway.) In contrast funeral processions of shahids attract enormous crowds. They offer an occasion to vent collective emotion, compassion, anger. They rekindle community ties in a kindred spirit of anguish and pain. A moderate university professor explained this to me in the following terms : " I have been to funerals of Hamas militants. We pay our respects to families we would not normally socialise with. It is our tradition. " Sally, whose position is more political and less Palestinian, says : " Those people chose suicide stupidly ; I refuse to shed tears for them. "

After consulting different sources I learn that shahid, a religious term commonly translated as martyr, applies to a person who dies in battle, whatever the circumstances of death. In literal translation shahid means " witness " because every deceased person meets God. The term can also be translated as hero or victim.

In the early afternoon I am with Firas, a young civil servant in the Palestinian Ministry of Culture. We are on our way to the site of yesterday's fighting. Actually Firas would rather sit with me in a cosy café and talk about the contemporary Egyptian novel, his recently completed Ph.D.. Or we could discuss the French novel or the question of realism in writing. Firas is responsible for publishing at the Ministry.

" We print a wide variety of publications, but we avoid religion. We leave that to the private sector. My position involves reception of manuscripts, reading them and organising reviews by various committees. " Firas is also a writer and leader of writers' workshops. I thought he might take a personal interest in seeing where the fighting took place. " If you insist, but for us, it's everyday life. We've become accustomed to death and destruction. " I'm not convinced. Arguably, Ramallah was invaded several times in 2002 and placed under lengthy curfews in March, April and September. There were fewer deaths than in Nablus and Jenin, because the local resistance in Ramallah was weak. Since my arrival the army has made only one large-scale incursion into Ramallah resulting in a single death (a newly wed young man who happened to be passing by). Another person – a twenty-eight year old lawyer who lived in the neighbourhood – was killed while handling a suicide belt. With the four deaths yesterday the total number of dead in two months is six. These grim statistics place Ramallah far behind Sarajevo or Beirut. The daily lot here may indeed be humiliation, lawlessness and uncertainty ; it is not death.

Could it be that Firas has lost all curiosity, all desire to observe with his own eyes what is happening in his city ? Is his denial an attempt to protect himself from events that shake him more deeply than they do me ? Firas wears a dark overcoat and leather gloves. His features are delicate. He is a refined young man and hails from a well-to-do Muslim family. A member of the elite, he was educated at the very best Christian schools in Bethlehem and at the University of Cairo. His soft leather moccasins are not at all suited to the ochre-coloured mud that spills through the streets we trudge through. As we discuss literature under the protection of his umbrella, we make our way to our destination in one of Ramallah's most residential neighbourhoods, less than a hundred metres from the Lutheran Church and the Sakakini Cultural Centre. The four-storey building, in which one of the militants hid, is completely demolished. It is a mere pile of rubble that draws curious onlookers on their way back from the funeral. Children climb gingerly through the ruins, as the plumbing continues to vomit its contents.

A little girl with long curly black hair and a small boy wearing a red cap are standing on the balcony of a neighbouring building. They invite us up. There are large cracks in the walls. The iron bars on the windows are smashed. Rubble from the ceiling deposits a layer of dust and dirt everywhere ; windows and mirrors are shattered. What words can I offer to these children who show me their beds full of plaster and stones ; their stuffed animals lying among the shards of glass ; the broken computer in a corner of the boy's room ; the kitchen and bathroom ruined ; the broken ceiling with brownish rain waters seeping through. Silently I take picture after picture. Their father and older brother join us. They explain to Firas what happened. Firas translates.

Sunday around ten p.m. the army arrived on the scene with dozens of armoured vehicles. Sharp shooters took up positions in the surrounding buildings. They evacuated the residents and held the women and children in one flat, men in another. Some of the women cried ; the men were interrogated. Residents and visitors were held from ten that evening until ten the following morning. Shots were heard throughout the night. In the buildings the Israelis occupied many of the windows have been shot out. Helicopters provided cover for the entire operation. Monday noon soldiers placed dynamite in every room of some twenty flats ; then blew them up.

Thirteen-year-old Ayya, her features drawn, sheds not one tear. She has hardly slept since Sunday. Her seven-year-old brother does not cry. Neither her older brother nor her father. With gloomy faces they show us around, taking us through rooms now exposed to the elements, accepting that we take pictures. On a mirror in the parents' bedroom we see a name in the thick dust : " Kiswani ", the family that owns this building and a few others, including the one completely demolished. Palestinians compare the Israeli occupation to rape. I feel the same about taking pictures of their ruined home. It is time to leave.

What do Ayya and her brother know about the men the Israelis were after ? " They were guests, not residents of the building. " Hospitality is a sacred value, even if the price is the loss of one's home.

In another country regrets would be expressed, but not here. The surrender of the militant would not have saved the building from demolition. Israeli policy* has been to systematically destroy any house suspected of harbouring a terrorist. This is carried out before the very eyes of the residents of the premises in order to induce submission.

In the late afternoon the shutters of all shops are still closed. " They have to stay closed ", Firas

---

* On February 17, 2005 the Israeli Minister of Defence announced a cessation of punitive house demolitions. From October 2001 to January 2005 Israel demolished 668 homes in the Occupied Territories as punishment. Source : B'Tselem.

explains. " It's the custom. Curtains must remain drawn when a funeral procession passes by. It's a sign of respect for the dead. Sure, it's something of an exaggeration to keep them closed all day. But the head of the Intifada insists on them being closed. " At night fall the food shops raise their shutters halfway and let in a few customers.

Ohaila, a young feminist activist I know, was held with the women and children in the flat Sunday night. " One woman never stopped moaning about the expensive new clothes she had just purchased. "

Jalal Khader, a lawyer, occupied a flat in the demolished building. " I was in my pyjamas when the soldiers ordered us to come out. They asked me if I knew a certain person, but I had never heard the name. He was probably lodging with another tenant that I had seen maybe three times. The whole building belongs to the Kiswani family ; they have fifteen children or so. Six of the flats were rented. We heard shots, but it was impossible to tell if it was the Israelis who were shooting or if shots were coming from the other building as well. We read in the newspaper that a police dog carrying a camera had been injured. Monday morning, one person per flat was allowed fifteen minutes to collect a few personal belongings. By that time there was nobody left in the building, otherwise they wouldn't have allowed us back in. I recovered my passport and my portable computer. That's all. After that the Israelis blew up the building. The governor of Ramallah has offered us a thousand US dollars in compensation. I have a mind to refuse the money. Tuesday the Palestinian security forces found a body in a plastic tub in the ruins of another building. Had the Israelis perhaps stashed the body there ? Nobody knows. In any case, none of us saw anyone coming out of our building. "

I had met this lawyer- anthropologist on several occasions already. I appreciate Jalal Khader 's concern for detail.

The wildest rumours circulate here. A friend gives us news of five deaths in the Amari refugee camp, supposedly four in the street. Closer to the fact, it is three adults, probably Hamas militants, found dead in two separate buildings (the circumstances of their deaths remain unclear) and a child hit by a stray bullet during the demonstration in the camp.

Seeing Jalal Khader here again, I find him completely changed, and not just because he is wearing a simple pullover instead of his elegant blue marine suit with silk tie and gold cufflinks. He is troubled, even shocked, that his building was completely demolished, though no suspect was found, which means there was no reason for it. " I can't get the child out of my mind begging for his schoolbag so he can go to school, or the old woman asking for the dentures she left in her flat. I am willing to give the Israelis whatever they want – settlements, land, whatever – as long as they take responsibility for all the suffering they have caused us since 1948 ! I will never give in on this point. " Two months ago Jalal Khader believed in the two state solution. He told me then : " The day we have our own state, I will do anything to stop the terrorist attacks, even if it means becoming a policeman or a border guard. " That seems so long ago now.

Wednesday. The weather is glorious. I will try to travel to Tulkarm though it is currently under a harsh Israeli lock down. Perhaps on the way I will catch a close-up glimpse of the infamous concrete Wall. I reach Surda checkpoint mid-morning and witness an extraordinary scene. Cordons of Israeli soldiers have blocked huge throngs of people at each end of the no-man's land. Army bulldozers are busy re-opening the passage. They clear away huge mounds of earth and heavy stone bollards which had been placed there not long ago to block traffic. Television cameras cover the event as press photographers scramble up and down the obstacles. No doubt the operation is part of the same plan that Ariel Sharon announced to his American allies recently. In sum, a gesture of appeasement. True, the roadblock had no impact on Israeli security, because the north road leads only to Nablus, Jenin, Tulkarm and Jericho. It does not even occupy a strategic crossroads. It merely blocks access to Ramallah, paralysing commerce and industry, poisoning the life of Bir Zeit University, spoiling the lives of twenty thousand people, who every day have to leave taxis at the first point, walk eight hundred metres, and find another taxi on the other side, all of this in absolute chaos. The only winners at this game are the street hawkers, who peddle their fruit and vegetables, pots and pans, socks and CD's, and of course the drivers of horse carts who ferry across merchandise and less spry pedestrians.

On her way to university Malika went through the checkpoint later in the day and witnessed the farewell of the horse cart drivers. Before returning to their villages with their worn-out hacks, they burst into patriotic and popular song.

On the other side of the rapidly disappearing checkpoint I find a seat in a bus ; it fills little by little, primarily with male Palestinian travellers. The more unsafe travel conditions become, the fewer the women. The bus ticket to Tulkarm costs ten shekels, considerably less than a taxi. And the journey is much faster, too, because the itinerary is simpler. On certain stretches the bus is able to travel on the same road that soldiers and settlers use to reach the Jewish settlements of Ariel and Emmanuel. But it is only allowed to stop in Arab towns and villages. Road signs show Tel Aviv to be only forty kilometres away. It's hard to believe. It is a landscape of rock-strewn hills planted with olive trees. In the Arab villages, where everything seems aimlessly adrift, road signs are in Hebrew as well. One feels the burden of colonisation. In Anabta, a village before Tulkarm, the bus releases most passengers. Only four of us remain with the driver. I strike up a conversation with a fifty-year-old man dressed like a businessman. Imad is an economist with a degree from Prague University. He is currently studying the economic impact of the Wall on Tulkarm and the surrounding region. He works for the Palestinian Authority in Ramallah and returns home to his family in Tulkarm every Wednesday. " If you have any problems with the soldiers and they won't let you cross to the other side, you are welcome to stay at my home. Here is my telephone number. " Palestinian hospitality never fails.

On the outskirts of Tulkarm the military construction works are visible everywhere. Over several kilometres bulldozers have cut down trees. Heavy lorries plough through the reddish ochre mud. The bus stops ; a soldier boards to check the documents of the vehicle and passengers. He looks at my passport and pauses, but does not ask what I'm doing here. In principle, tourists are not allowed and I am not on official assignment. Perhaps my white hair inspires trust. He leaves the bus without further comment. Directly in front of the bus some fifty peasants on foot or donkey attempt to leave the city. They show their documents to soldiers who treat them roughly, lifting blankets and packsaddles with their weapons to inspect vegetables. An old peasant woman, wearing a traditional broidered garment and veil, endures inspection on the back of a donkey. Her wrinkled face shows a tired, weary expression. In Palestinian eyes, no scene is more revolting than a twenty-year-old soldier treating an old woman rudely. " I'd rather stay home than witness such a thing. It makes me mad for weeks " a neighbour once told me. The small crowd waits its turn behind the barrier and watches hopelessly. Humiliation, imprisonment, misery : a summary of the occupation.

On the other side of the checkpoint it is almost possible to breathe again. One enters a lively city with small gardens and terraces covered in vines. Children in their UNRWA uniforms walk home from school. Markets are teeming with victuals, household goods, clothing and basic commodities. In the high street, as in every Palestinian city, the dozen or so jewellery shops display their gold articles in the window : chains, rings and bracelets gifted as dowry to future spouses. At the foot of the mosque a farmer sells lettuce from a donkey cart, like the one the soldiers were inspecting earlier at the checkpoint ; the donkey is still harnessed to it. Before the Intifada the market was three or four times larger ; Jews and Arabs from Israel came every weekend to purchase fruit and vegetables at unbeatable prices. A trio of schoolgirls, books tucked under their arms, dressed in Islamic fashion – long coats buttoned down to their shoes, tightly knotted headscarves – show me the road leading west to the Israeli military post. It is still known as the DCO (District Coordination Office) in memory of the fleeting period when Israelis and Palestinians cooperated in maintaining order. " It's too far to walk ", they say, " Take a taxi. " I follow their advice. The taxi heads down the hill, skirts the University and crosses a former industrial zone. The concrete wall in the distance blocks the horizon completely. As we approach the military post the condition of the road worsens markedly ; the landscape is sinister : barbed wire, potholes, abandoned hangars. The taxi driver drops me off, quickly turns around and, before speeding away, signals to me to continue straight ahead, towards the building site, access to which is closed by a large yellow metal barrier. I approach the site, but some soldiers shout something that does not sound very friendly. I backtrack and enter the cement courtyard of the DCO. At least fifty Palestinians stand at wired windows. Distress and confusion everywhere. They request travel or building permits that will probably be denied. Standing on the roof, a soldier with wild hair and unkempt beard barks an order for me to go back where I came from. The place is too frightening to risk taking a picture. Another soldier approaches the yellow barrier. Do I speak Hebrew ? Not a word. Russian ? Yes, that's better. From a distance he shouts : " What are you doing here ? Open your bag. " I move closer, my hands in the air, my passport in one hand and my bag in the other. Now I'm at the yellow barrier, only a metre from him. He's a short man with cropped blond hair, helmet pulled down hard, muscles like a gymnast. He pages through my passport, pulls out a twenty euro bill and hands it to me with a wry smile. (God forbid I should attempt to corrupt anyone. I have no idea how the bill found its way into my passport.) His Uzi pointed at me (honestly, I just can't get used to these things), he enquires in Russian : " What are you doing here ? Are you a reporter ? – No, I'm a writer. – Ah. Do you have a permit ? A professional card ? – Writers don't need one. – Of course they do ! Where are you from ? – From Ramallah. – Before that ? – Paris. And you, you weren't born in Israel, were you ? – No, I'm from Odessa. – I'd love to visit the Black Sea. A few years ago I went hiking in the Caucuses. – Where ? – Mount Elbrouz. Have you been there ? – OK. You can pass. Keep straight. Don't step off to the left or right. Right through there. "

At times like this I'm glad I had Russian in school. I trudge fifty metres along a muddy path through a building site, which ends abruptly at the Wall. Its towering grey slabs, nearly fifty centimetres thick, are held together by giant rivets ; they stretch left and right for kilometres on end, higher than prison walls. I dare not reach for my camera. Watchful soldiers observe my every step ; video surveillance cameras are everywhere. On the other side of the Wall, the contrast is striking, again the torn curtain. I am confronted with a Western four-lane highway stretching north and south the length of Israel. A man-made slope has been created on the Israeli side to hide the Wall. Landscape artists have set out to make it nice, green, harmless. I hitch a ride fifteen kilometres to a busy intersection just before Netanya, the coastal city between Tel Aviv and Haifa. Distances in Israel/Palestine are ridiculously small. The more I travel in this handkerchief of barbed wire and security fences, the less I believe in the future coexistence of two states.

A young blonde-headed soldier confirms in English that this is where the Jerusalem-bound 647 bus stops. " What are you doing here ? Are you a tourist ? – Not exactly. I'm a writer. – No kidding. So am I. Short stories, poems, songs. " In the bus he gives me one of his songs to read. " Like a fallen star…where are the friends from long ago, from days of old and happier times ? Now I'm in a fix, I'm in a bind and have my troubles…like a fallen star, like a fallen star. " He's happy with the lyrics, but he's still working on the music. He hopes to make a recording in the US soon. We spend the next hour and a half side by side in conversation. It's very informative. Here is the gist of it.

Daniel is from San Diego. His parents didn't get along. He was a high school drop out and fell to using drugs. At twenty-one he " went up to Israel " (as the expression goes) and for three years buried himself in religion. He's not married yet. He joined the army " to serve his country " (again, as the expression goes). Daniel is proud to be a Cohen, of rabbinical lineage. Like all Jews – in his words " ninety percent, scientifically proven " – he is a direct blood descendant of Abraham ; his duty is to marry a Jewish woman to perpetuate the bloodline. He follows the ancient laws of his Hebrew ancestors, who received them directly from God. These laws are above the laws of any state and, of course, the UN. He finished his military service but is currently serving a period in the reserves.

" Do you like the army ?

– Being a soldier teaches togetherness. It makes me feel useful. Anyway, we have to control Arabs with an iron fist, like primary school kids. If we let them off the hook, things will get out of hand. Besides they're liars. It's not worth talking with them. We've tried everything. They don't want our state. Before we had it, they attacked us constantly. They killed a Jewish obstetrician, who provided free care for Arab women for years. They raped his wife and daughter in front of his eyes.

– Palestinians probably tell the same stories about the Jews.

– So, you're on their side, are you !

– Nationalism is not my cup of tea. It matters to me as much as the latest football scores. You think that being born Jewish is the most important thing in your life. Not me. OK, it's part of our heritage, but we all belong to the human race. We are all tenants of the same planet. Really, don't you find it a bit narrow to look at the world through the history of a small nation of only twelve million ?

– Well, for one, we'd be at least twenty-four million, except for the Shoah. Anyway, whoever took our side during the Shoah ? During the Inquisition ? During the Black Plague ? No one. So why should we care about other people today ? Besides, you French, you only hate the English and the Americans because they took your colonies. You don't even speak English. I can't believe I've been talking with you all this time... But since you're French, let me ask you a question : do you think I can have sex before I get married ?

144

– Where's the problem ? If you and your partner agree, why not ? But why do you think you have to get married ? Personally I don't think marriage is for everyone.

– But I have to get married, so my children are Jewish. Anyway I have to go back to the US to make some money, because here, with the Jews, it's really hard to do business. "

Traffic jams, rain ; as we come closer to Jerusalem the roads are more crowded. Daniel has been quiet for a while ; now he prepares to say good-bye.

" This evening I'm going to try to win some money at the slot machines. I lost a lot in the army. After that I'll meet with some friends at a bar, then I'll go see my girlfriend. By the way, what did you think of my song ? "

" It's ok. Don't worry. "

As you step off the bus, before going through the terminal, you have to show your passport again, open your bag. Again I see Palestinians showing their IDs (blue for residents of East Jerusalem), undergoing full body searches. I'll be glad to be back in Ramallah soon.

Here are a few more highlights from the week.

An election campaign to choose student delegates is in full swing on the Bir Zeit campus. They are the first elections in three years. In vain Fatah has tried to postpone them. The campaign is lively : musical processions, flags, multi-coloured banners, posters, stickers and big crowds at the noonday political meetings. It's a festive atmosphere : the different groups show respect for each other, patiently and courteously awaiting their turn at the microphone.

As far as the Geneva Understandings are concerned, Hamas and Fatah have virtually the same political position : both reject it outright and demand the right of return and Jerusalem as the capital. In addition, Hamas students demand the return of all land. Some parade by in suicide clothes, holding an open Qur'an to their chests.

With Malika, my neighbour, we watch this jeunesse doré, happy, excited, proud to vote for the first time. " I hope we maintain this freedom of speech for our students ", she says. " That's what's most important. " " And what do you think about the students who threw stones at the French Prime Minister ? " – I don't condemn them. Jospin's speech against Hamas and the terrorist organisations was out of place here in our country under occupation. I admit, the gesture was not pretty, but it was freedom of speech. – Is that what you really think ? ", I ask.

The election results come in Wednesday evening : twenty-five seats for Hamas, twenty for Fatah, six for the Left (an alliance of parties on the left and the People's Party). And Bir Zeit is the most liberal of the campuses in Palestine.

Tuesday, 9 December. Jane Birkin performs to a full house in the Al-Kassaba theatre. She is on a world tour, which includes Israel and the Occupied Territories (Gaza, Ramallah, Bethlehem) with her album Arabesques. The French Consul sees the opportunity to host a cocktail for the French-speaking community in Ramallah.

Thursday, 11 December. Another society event with an artistic political subtext is organised at the Qattan Cultural Centre. It is the opening of a video and photo exhibition entitled Chicpoint – Fashion for

146

Israeli Checkpoints. Shareef Waked, an Israeli Arab artist from Haifa, has produced a video of a subversive all male catwalk. The models are dark, handsome Mediterranean types with plastered down hair. A heavy cotton shirt highlights the midriff with loosely woven netting ; a white shirt with peek through holes reveals the abdomen ; a casual jacket incorporates a zipper at the waist. The fashion concept is simple : because all men have to bare their stomachs at checkpoints, to prove they are not wearing explosive belts, sexy, truculent and overstated designs mockingly expose flesh and body parts. The seven-minute video concludes with recent documentary photos showing men lifting their shirts for soldiers at checkpoints. Some, blindfolded, are shirtless, others fully naked.

To conclude these chronicles here are some quick replies to a few questions my friends in Paris send me.

" As a Jew, do you feel safe in the Occupied Territories ? – Yes "

" Do people know you are Jewish ? – Those who ask know. But nobody has created any trouble for me on this issue. Nobody has said, since you're Jewish, explain to me why…Never. And nobody has ever asked to see what I write, not even to check any quotes I attribute to them. "

" What do you mean exactly by checkpoint ? – A military roadblock that everyone goes through either on foot, in a vehicle or on a donkey. The West Bank has several hundred checkpoints now. During curfews they are always closed and Palestinians are confined to residence. Under " normal " circumstances of the occupation, opening and closing times are fairly unpredictable. The aim is to block Palestinian access to Israel, the Jewish colonies, military zones, strategic highways, water tanks, and the cities and towns where armed resistance is strong (Jenin, Nablus), indeed any location deemed " sensitive ". In practice, as a territory, Palestine is now pretty much an archipelago of " enclaves " with no easy internal passage. "

" Do Palestinian men have several wives ? – Not in Ramallah. In general polygamy is on the decline. There is residual evidence of it in Gaza and in some villages. No more than four percent. "

" Do Palestinian suicide bombers, like Al-Qaeda members, believe that they will be rewarded in Heaven with seventy-two virgins as Muhammad promised ? – Given the efficiency of Shin Beit I doubt there is a single Al-Qaeda activist in Palestine. I have no idea what the Qur'an promises and no idea what the Prophet vowed to female bombers. But most observers admit that occupied Palestine has an unlimited supply of suicide candidates. The choice available to sponsors of terrorism is large, embarrassingly so. "

12 – 24 December

Lately my chronicles have become more spread out in time. You should not conclude from this, dear Reader, that there is less to see, less to hear or learn here, or that I now find the circumstances simply normal and ordinary. The fact is my life is less solitary at present ; friends are staying with me for the next ten days. With Gerard, a philosopher, we spend time discussing the notions of " the people " (the terms " Jewish people " and " Palestinian people " are not symmetrical) ; sovereignty (two states, one state, what sovereignty ?) ; " state of exception " (laws governing colonised or occupied populations) ; " body of exception " (a reference to the colonised subject who is considered dangerous less for his acts or his ideas, but for his offspring)…

Since December 23rd a small camera team is working here to create a documentary film from my chronicles. What pictures and words are able to express planned asphyxiation, erratic violence and the absolute arbitrariness of the situation here ? My friends and I walk from one end of Hebron to the other, its historical centre slowly being killed by settlers and soldiers. Then, on New Year's Eve we crisscross Nablus, still under siege, surrounded by tanks and armoured vehicles. For these reasons, my chronicle will momentarily take the drier tone of a diary, a few notes scribbled on the run.

12 December. Friday. Bright and warm. The city sleeps. An urge to take a walk in the countryside. Walking south, beyond Al-Manara Square, one passes through dirty streets lined with houses of uncertain architecture. The tiny courtyards are cluttered with rubbish. Children scramble up and down heaps of rubble. Young boys loiter around the Internet café. Inside a dozen more pursue virtual enemies through an urban landscape of high-rise towers set somewhere in America. This is the Qaddura refugee camp, a three hundred metre square enclave near the city centre and main market. It has never been officially recognised by the United Nations as a camp. As a result, the residents do not have access to UNRWA services ; there is no school, no hospital dispensary. Qaddura ranks as no more than a poor area of the city surrounded by more prosperous districts. I receive these explanations from a medical doctor who comes to the Internet café to collect his son. Mohammed Haddad was born in the camp and grew up there. He learned French in Lyons where he spent two years as an intern studying chronic diseases. Currently he works for Medical Relief, a Palestinian community-based health organisation. He points out the house he recently built, directly across from the Internet café, on the street that separates the camp from the city of Ramallah. The charming little house has a small

150

courtyard and garden with pergola. Built on the edge of the camp, it expresses the agonizing indecision of the refugees. Even those who have the means to leave the camp are unable to make the break ; it would represent abandonment and betrayal. To leave the camp is to walk away from one's family, one's childhood friends, and a large part of one's hopes and commitments. Dr. Mohammed Haddad chooses to live an in-between zone. Other refugees and sons of refugees build nice flats within the camp perimeter, in the middle of the slum.

Continuing south one enters Al-Bireh, the twin city of Ramallah. Historically, Al-Bireh was Muslim and Ramallah was Christian. Today nothing distinguishes one from the other. The new districts developing in a southerly direction are uniformly middle class. Large residential buildings have white limestone facades ; here and there palm trees adorn the streets and, at crossroads, one finds the occasional supermarket. A florist has set out rows of palm, lemon, orange and laurel trees of all shapes and sizes. A wide avenue with a median strip leads to the most luxurious hotel of the district, the Grand Park Hotel. A few hundred metres further the city dissolves into the countryside and becomes farmland, olive trees, heaths and a wasteland of abandoned vehicles. An old peasant woman in a heavy black dress with red embroidery hoes a miniscule plot of land. Further down the road a quarry comes into view. There are deep ruts carved by the wheels of heavy lorries to wade through. Though it is Friday a few workers are busy in a cement and brick factory. In the distance one catches a glimpse of the " Iron Curtain ". Here it takes the form of a two lane highway lined with lacerating barbed wire ; every fifty metres there are red signs in three languages : " military zone – crossing or damaging the fence is at the risk of your life ". On the other side of this virtual border one sees the Arab suburbs of Jerusalem doomed for annexation.

No Israeli patrol is visible on the road, but the young workers at the cement factory caution us : " Stay away from the road. The Israelis shoot and ask questions later. " I read that five children from the nearby Kalandia refugee camp were killed near the barbed wire fence recently. Today, in broad daylight, with the sun shining, the risk seems minimal, all the more so that a shepherd and his son are guarding their flock of sheep and goats, grazing in a field behind the cement works. The father wearing a white keffiyeh waves a greeting. He poses with his son for the camera, then gives us a mobile phone number where he can be reached.

Three days later the Grand Park Hotel welcomes a delegation of Italian businessmen led by a minister of the Berlusconi government. After the banquet lunch, during which they promise to develop joint investments with Palestinian entrepreneurs (the same promise they made a day earlier to the Israelis), before driving back to the airport in Tel Aviv under military escort, the elegantly dressed businessmen in dark suits with silk ties pose for official and unofficial pictures in the warm sun on the hotel terrace. Evidently no one notices the impassable highway obstructing the horizon.

Saturday. 13 December. Israel's extreme left parties call a demonstration in support of A-Ram, a neighbourhood that is protesting the Wall. It is a shambles, fenced in on two sides by barbed wire, to the north by the Kalandia refugee camp and Atarot airport, to the south by Beit Hanina. Soon A-Ram will be entirely cut off from Jerusalem. Around eleven a.m. a high polystyrene wall is erected along the Jerusalem–Ramallah highway at the level of a petrol station. By noon the local youth have cheerfully kicked it to pieces. The crowd is not large, perhaps two thousand people at most. I recognise several Israeli activists I met in October at the olive harvest. As for Palestinians, the crowd is mixed : a few high school students on their way back home, several dozen more youths perched on the roof of the petrol station. A podium has been improvised on the flat bed of a lorry ; speeches are delivered in Arabic and Hebrew. Here is the gist. This Wall, which cuts off Palestinian neighbourhoods from other Palestinian neighbourhoods, will disrupt everyday life and make it even more chaotic than it already is. Dozens of villages to the west of the new " Great Wall " are already suffocating ; the cities of Qalqiliya and Tulkarm are in a stranglehold. Each day, little by little, Palestinians are being pushed back and imprisoned in increasingly isolated ghettos. The economy is collapsing ; more and more obstacles spring up along routes leading to schools and universities. Access to hospitals is totally unpredictable. As usual Uri Avnery talks to television reporters and answers their questions. He assails the " Wall of Apartheid ", denouncing it as a crime against humanity. He appeals to his fellow Israeli citizens, and to international opinion in general, to wake up and protest more vigorously. By one thirty p.m. the Israeli activists are back in their buses and on their way home to Tel Aviv and Haifa. Distraught, the Palestinian demonstrators trudge home on foot.

I return on foot as well, walking through A-Ram from one end to the other along the high street lined with shops. I see the usual fruit and vegetable shops, but also shops selling light fixtures, building materials and tools ; there are automobile repair shops, second-hand goods traders, appliance sellers and huge quantities of rubbish thrown haphazardly by the wayside. At the end of the road I see more barbed wire and another no man's land. In the distance there are five or six soldiers guarding the building site around the Iron Curtain. The project involves thousands. Not long ago it was still possible to avoid the checkpoint by slipping down into this small gully and through some undergrowth. Now soldiers pace back and forth with heavy feet.

Monday. 15 December. The film producer Raed Andoni drops by for a visit. We drink a few beers and watch videos from Paris. He strikes me as gloomy and exhausted. " I'm thirty-six years old. I'll never be thirty-five again. I can never forgive them for stealing my youth ; for depriving me of happiness forever. " When we talk about the future, Raed returns to what he told me two months ago : " I don't believe there will be a just peace. Not as long as Israel defines itself as a Jewish state. We can live together only if Israel accepts to become not only a democratic state, but also a secular state, for all of its citizens, for all of the people who live there, regardless of their religious origins. This is the necessary framework for resolving the three problems of the refugees, the Arab Israelis and Jerusalem. "

Raed's family lives in Bethlehem where it owns land. Land doesn't mean much to me. As far back as my genealogy can be traced there are no landowners among my ancestors. In fact, there is nowhere I can call the land of my ancestors, not Russia, not Lithuania, not Germany, not Alsace. I can only claim a few square (or cubic) metres in a Jewish cemetery near Paris. But for Raed it is different. " Whenever my mother has some money, she buys a parcel of land. For her, and for my entire family, land has genuine value. Even when some of her land is confiscated, she tells herself there will always be something left. But when I go to Bethlehem, I really don't feel part of the community anymore. "

Land. If we are to believe Jeff Halper, an Israeli anthropologist who leads the Committee Against House Demolitions, Israel has already expropriated twenty-four percent of the West Bank, eighty-nine percent of East Jerusalem and twenty-five percent of Gaza (including land for settlements, roads, security areas and military zones).

Tuesday. 16 December. The Christian cemetery in Ramallah. The graves lie side-by-side in the shade of cypresses and pines. The headstones bear carved crosses and inscriptions, some in Arabic, some in English. Some steles display grave portraits based on an identity photo. Wealthier families indulge in luxurious burial vaults complete with lions (the same statues guarding Al-Manara Square). Most families are content with tiny plots, which proliferate even in the cemetery's paths. There is simply not enough space. The municipality of Ramallah plans to expand the cemetery, but the new land is in Zone C requiring a permit from the Israeli " civilian " authorities. The permit is systematically refused. As a result, it is often necessary to exhume the remains of the " old dead " to make room for the " new ". Even Christian, even dead, Palestinian Arabs seem unwanted in their land. Zyad Khalaf provides these explanations. He is the director of the Qattan Foundation, a cultural centre with modern facilities (it has a tastefully furnished library, exhibition space, and a residence for writers and artists). It sits adjacent to the cemetery. Thanks to generous contributions from wealthy patrons, the Foundation conducts a wide range of cultural activities featured on a modern website.

Zyad Khalaf, fifty years old, an engineer by training, has lived in the United States and in the United Kingdom. It pains him, he tells me, that there have been too many dead, " way too many dead ". He no longer has the heart to attend the funerals of these young people, " much too young to die ". His phone never stops ringing. " The funerals attract fewer people today. The Intifada itself is dead. The popular insurrection is dead. We have been crushed under the weight of repression. Since the beginning of the Occupation thirty-five years ago, over six hundred thousand Palestinians have been arrested and imprisoned. One in ten Palestinian males have spent time in prison. This is where we stand. " He is currently building a family house ; the architectural plans lie on his desk. How is he coping with the Occupation ? " I am angry, frustrated, frightened. I constantly ask myself, why does it have to be like this ? The only answer I've been able to find for myself is work and family. I turn things over in my mind. I've reached the conclusion that we can't relinquish our rights ; that path would be wrong for everyone, for us and for others. A denial of justice will never lead to a long-term solution. From this point of view the Geneva Understandings were a big mistake. Israel must recognise the atrocities it has committed. "

Wednesday. 17 December. I finish an article for a French NGO, La Ligue des droits de l'homme*. They asked me to summarise in three pages how the past three months in occupied Palestine have shifted my ideas.

Completely absorbed in writing – which is my way of thinking through the issues – I missed my appointment with Ilan Halevi at the Ministry of Foreign Affairs. As a result I idled away my time in the north of the city between the Muqataa and Beit El, the Israeli military post, where most of the government offices are located. There is a huge American-style shopping mall inaugurated last year and a hamam, whose virtues I praised above.

Thursday. 18 December. Ilan Halevi offers me a catch-up session at eleven a.m.. It must be short because he is leaving for a month, to France first, then to Mumbai and the World Social Forum, where he will represent Palestine officially.

Ilan Halevi is worth a portrait. His physique would captivate a Velasquez, his courage a Malraux or a Camus. I first met him in the courtyard of the Muqataa with Uri Averny and others on the evening of October 5th. That evening his conversation was pleasant and very witty. Today, at the end of the morning seated at his desk, he is much the same, and a bit of a charmer as well. Erudite, he is obviously a

---

professional politician ; a talented writer as well, as his recent book, *Face à la guerre, lettre de Ramallah*[*], attests.

" An entirely just peace is impossible. At best we will reach agreement on a mutually acceptable basis and hope that, in time, conditions will become more favourable. "

As a member of the PLO leadership and personal advisor to Arafat he wants to believe that a realistic compromise will succeed. But the present circumstances are bleak.

The alternative to war is a compromise between might and right. But Palestinians no longer believe in the willingness of Israel to compromise. After three years of violence, our society is on a knife's edge. As a result Palestinians cling strictly to the terms of their rights. The thinking goes like this : since the Israelis oppose every one of our claims, we might as well keep them all on the table. This is the same attitude that Palestinians from Israel expressed earlier when they rejected all proposals for compensation. "

Moderately optimistic :

" Since the official announcement of the Geneva Understandings, public support has diminished in Israel and in Palestine. The latest West Bank opinion polls show thirty percent in favour, thirty percent against and forty percent undecided. On both sides no more than a third of the population is prepared to support a quick solution to the conflict.

" Anyway a final agreement between the two sides will merely sanction the existing power balance. And in my opinion time is running out for Palestinians. Our society is weakening dramatically.

---

[*] In French, Sindbad-Actes Sud, 2003.

" Israelis are pulling back from a final agreement for a variety of reasons, not the least of which is the fetishizing of the Shoah. The movement towards democracy will not happen on its own but will require international pressure. In the meantime Israel is plunging ever deeper into an institutionalisation of the denial of citizenship for Palestinians. "

Ilan Halevi was born into a communist family in 1943 in Lyons. When he was twenty-two years old he moved to Israel-Palestine. " When my mother heard of my plans to settle here, she worried I had become a Zionist. I quickly reassured her. My father was a Yemeni Jew whose family settled in Jerusalem at the beginning of the century. The Sephardim were so unwelcoming that the Yemeni community settled outside the walls of the city in the village of Silwan. The neighbourhood has since been absorbed into the suburbs of Jerusalem. If circumstances dictate that I must be presented for what I was at birth – rather than for what I became (a Palestinian militant, a writer and a leader of the movement) – then I would say I am first an Arab, then a Jew. People perform incredible language contortions to avoid the term Arab Jew. They speak of Oriental Jews, Yemini, Moroccan and Tunisian Jews. But we are, of course, Arab by language, culture and custom. "

In the late afternoon I pick up Gerard and Pierrette at Ben Gourion International Airport. Outside the icy rain turns almost to snow as the taxi climbs the road back to Ramallah.

Friday. 19 December. More rain, fog and cold. At the Kalandia checkpoint a sewer worker's boots would be precious. Sari Hanafi has invited us to a meeting of the Palissade group to be held in East

Jerusalem in the offices of a Palestinian association. Fifteen Palestinian and Israeli professors are seated around the table, including the historian Ilan Pappe (University of Haifa). The discussions are in English tainted with Arabic, Hebrew, German and American accents. The comments on the Geneva Understandings, the first item on this morning's agenda, make it quite impossible for a profane ear to determine which camp the different protagonists belong to. Most have serious reservations, running the full gamut to outright rejection. Some argue the case for a " yes, but ". Presiding over the session, Sari Hanafi declares " the Geneva Understandings offer the advantage that they stimulated a democratic debate on the Palestinian side ". Moshe Zuckerman, professor of Germanic Studies at the University of Tel Aviv, declares " I personally dream of a Middle East without states. But in pragmatic terms, it is probably better to use all available resources to free ourselves from the dead-end situation we are in now. " Others offer analysis of the more controversial paragraphs of the Accord. Do the Understandings include recognition of Israel as the Jewish state ? Not exactly. The formulation expresses " the right of the Jewish people to a state ", something quite different.

In the opinion of Salim Tamari (department of sociology, Bir Zeit University), " this is a peripheral agreement between people on the margins of power ; it sells the Palestinian right of return for a very low price. "

As for Ilan Pappe, he refuses to be drawn into a discussion of the text of the Understandings. " First, because the end of occupation is not the end of the conflict. The text is presented to Israeli public opinion

160

as if it were historical reconciliation. That is a lie. The quality of the individuals promoting this text on the Israeli side should be proof enough to alert us to the dangers. Their racist arguments about the "demographic threat" are outrageous. In fact, the debate about Geneva only sidetracks us from the more urgent struggle, which is to oppose the Separation Wall. Geneva is a mere side-show, masking reality and sowing illusion. "

In the opinion of Issam Nassar, a Palestinian sociologist currently teaching in the United States, the text " makes no reference whatsoever to the events of the past three years. It claims to offer reconciliation but that will not happen for another generation or two. In essence, it offers nothing but Palestinian justification of Zionist goals ! "

Gerard, my friend from France (I am his interpreter during the meeting), is impressed at the courteousness, respectfulness and courtesy that is predominant around the table. Each participant makes an effort to keep his remarks short and to avoid repetition. Tension is rife between the ultras and moderates of both camps ; but nothing that might lead to rupture. During the coffee-cigarette-sandwich break small groups form according to affinity and by no means according to national belonging.

The second item on the agenda, the boycott of Israeli institutions of higher education, reveals further lines of division. At the origin of the initiative, the Palestinians from Bir Zeit University continue to encourage the boycott. Some of the Israelis at the table point out that the colleagues most affected by the boycott are those working in the social sciences, precisely those who are most critical of Israeli government action and policy. In comparison, the technological and scientific sectors, which are closest to army and government circles, are hardly touched at all. In sum, the boycott is a double-edged sword. Most of the Israeli participants would like a more far-reaching boycott that would encompass all Israeli products and lead to an awakening of Israeli public opinion. Ilan Pappe concludes, " The political forces within Israel capable of bringing about a change in consensus are simply insufficient. Anyway, strong international pressure will be necessary. As for me, I am prepared to pay the price. "

As the meeting breaks up Reuven Kaminer, the eldest participant at the meeting, still endowed with the physique of an athlete, is very friendly. " My grandson is currently on trial with four other refuzniks. My son also refused to serve in the army during the war in Lebanon. Why don't you come to Jerusalem one evening for dinner. We can talk some more about the situation, if you like, and get to know each other better. My American accent ? I'm from Colorado ".

As night falls in Jerusalem we walk through the empty streets of the Old City. Rain. Sari Hanafi takes us to the terrace of the Austrian Hospice of the Holy Family for the amazing view, which takes in minarets, the Mount of Olives, the golden Dome of the Rock and the Al-Aqsa mosque. We spend a few minutes in the church of the Holy Sepulchre and hear a mass in an unfamiliar ritual. At the Wailing Wall we run into difficulties, because it is Shabbat and the electronic security devices have been deactivated. We undergo a manual search carried out by extremely unfriendly policemen. Gerard and Pierrette, soaking wet and uncomfortable, feel like voyeurs in this supermarket of religions. How fortunate the souvenir shops are closed. Friday evenings both Muslims and Jews take a rest. Only Christian shops remain open for business ; but since the Intifada tourism has dropped to a trickle.

On the return journey to the Kalandia checkpoint, conversation with a taxi driver. " I spent ten years in prison, between the age of sixteen and twenty-six, because I was a PLO militant. I took my high school diploma in prison. When I got out I went to the United States and earned a civil engineering degree. I came back to Palestine with the Oslo Agreement. I had no papers, only a driving licence. The other day they tried to take it away from me. I was with my six year old daughter, who kicked the soldier in the leg and told him to give the licence back. Is that how you raise your daughter the soldier asked. I replied, yes, I'm an aging PLO militant and my children will soon take over. " When we reach our destination, the taxi driver shakes my hand and refuses the money I offer for the fare.

24 December. Robin and Jean-Philippe arrive. Robin is a filmmaker, Jean-Philippe a musician. We run into some funny business at the Ministry of Interior that delivers professional accreditations. We are part of a production team, mere technical staff really, scheduled to make a documentary film on the archaeology of the Holy Places. The police officers tell us they have not received the necessary requests from Paris ; they instruct us to return in the afternoon. We find ourselves with some free time on our hands and in the grips of uncertainty. Will they double-check our cheeky declarations ? We walk around the Old City, then make our way west towards the well-off Jewish

districts near the King David Hotel and the YMCA. Gradually we near the neighbourhood where my grandmother lived : quiet streets lined with small buildings surrounded by gardens. No pedestrians, no cars, no shops : nothing in the atmosphere to suggest the Arab neighbourhoods we crossed moments earlier, except a few older houses in Ottoman style and the white stones that cover most facades. The empty lot, next to the Chopin street post office leading to my deceased grandmother's building, is still there, a fortunate escapee of urban renovation that has transformed this part of West Jerusalem into a vast retirement home for well-to-do Ashkenazi.

Ruth Katz, my grandmother's next-door neighbour for over thirty years, opens the door. She does not recognise me at first. I have not paid a visit for over ten years. Her face has finally succumbed to a few elegant wrinkles ; her hair is dyed blonde and pulled back into a bun. Still a virtuoso pianist ; still a prolific writer : four scholarly works on art and music published this year alone. She talks about her husband and the many awards he won in Israel, the United States and Europe. " Especially since the colleagues of his generation have started to pass away ", she adds almost spitefully. We trade family news, talk about grandchildren, nieces and nephews born in the past ten years. Watercolour and landscape paintings hang on the walls. " Your grandmother was such a character ", she says, " so we decided to keep her here in the flat. " In the dining room stands a life-size statue of an old woman dressed in mauve, unbelievably life-like, a near-perfect replica of my ancestor. The same corpulence, the same gloomy but determined expression, the same bell hat pulled down

164

over her ears, the same shawl, the same shopping bag in her hand, and the same low-heeled, round-toe shoes. " We found her in a New York art gallery and just couldn't resist. When the deliveryman opened the crate and saw the feet and legs, he had the fright of his life. He thought it was a corpse ! "

This life-like doll upsets me : I am in the presence of a copy of my grandmother made by an artist who never met her. When she died, Ruth and Eliaou Katz bought the two small rooms she lived in and enlarged their flat. Now both have their own office and the space seems even smaller than I remember. Do the bookshelves around the walls make it seem smaller or have I grown in the meantime ? I am momentarily caught up in family history. I was fourteen when I came to visit my grandmother in this building on Gdud Haivi for the first time. She had just moved in. My mother had passed away six years earlier, buried under suffocating silence. Have I come back perhaps to hold a conversation that was impossible at the time ? Only my grandmother ever spoke about my mother – or rather about the daughter she had lost ; a cheerful young girl, a bold adolescent, with whom she had left Brussels during the war and crossed the whole of occupied France before reaching London. They shared the most dangerous and the most heartbreaking moments together. She was inconsolable at the death of her daughter. But it is probable that she lost her before that, when she left London to marry my father ; or perhaps when my grandmother herself moved to Israel. Because it was all so very painful, charged with unconfessed secrets and a labyrinthine coil of guilt, my grandmother talked more about her other passion in life : Zionism. I did not share her passion, no doubt for reasons that were deeply personal and obscure.

Finally Ruth asks me what I am doing with a filmmaker and a musician in Israel. " It's good that you listen to the Palestinian side of the story, but don't forget the other side. You know, we don't share your grandmother's extremist ideas. We are against Sharon, but Arafat is a disaster. Why don't you come back for dinner some Friday evening so we can talk some more about the situation ? "

Before I can do that I must go to the cemetery and pay my respects at my grandmother's grave.

At the end of the afternoon we go back to the Ministry of Interior. The department head isn't really fooled by our yarn, but nonetheless he issues three temporary accreditations. Now we have the necessary permits to pass through certain checkpoints and grill Israeli soldiers with questions, camera and microphone firmly in hand.

The holidays have come and gone almost unnoticed. Christmas in Palestine is celebrated only by Christians, naturally, not all of them at the same time ; most follow the Gregorian calendar. Windows here have no Christmas garlands ; there are no twinkling stars hanging over streets. It is a family affair. My neighbours, Georgette and Malika, have set up Christmas trees in their flats. For the feast day of Santa Barbara they make a pudding with a sugary boulgour base containing nuts, raisins and almonds, flavoured with cinnamon and cloves, and decorated with sweetmeats. On the campus of Bir Zeit University, Christmas is more in evidence. A Christmas tree adorns the student cafeteria and students in Santa Claus outfits gambol between the buildings. They could be the same students who demonstrated two weeks ago in patriotic uniform (checked keffiyeh or black and green headbands).

The journey from Ramallah to Hebron (Al-Khalil in Arabic) now takes two to three hours ; before the Intifada, only one. The taxi, a beat-up, yellowish Mercedes that seats eight, swings to the east and around the agglomeration of Jerusalem. It passes through Bethlehem. It follows, more or less, the route of the Iron Curtain, which becomes a low wall as it cuts in half the main thoroughfare of Abu Dis, a suburb of East Jerusalem. Frequently obstructed by permanent or moving roadblocks, the road zigzags through the hills, climbs steep slopes and tumbles down into desert ravines. The morning sun skips over the rocks. Nomads have set up camp at the bottom of a small rocky gully. According to my tourist map of Israel – in fact, the only map of Palestine available – we are driving through the mountains of Judea. In the distance I see Jewish settlements ; some, like Maale Adumin, are already large towns. Perched on arid summits, the architecture and urban layout are European in style : sloped roofs covered with red tiles ; identical facades straight as a die ; hard lighting provided night and day by towering street lamps diffusing yellowish glare. The settlements are serviced by a network of roads and highways that are theoretically sealed off from the secondary roads travelled by Palestinians, when the army allows them to circulate at all. In times of tension, the army lowers the yellow barriers that are fitted on all important access routes and dump tons of rubble or dig deep trenches to make roads impassable. On this particular December 25th every road crossing has its guard post, barricade or watchtower ; Israeli soldiers filter the traffic. They salute drivers with a solemn boker tov (good morning in Hebrew) and beg a cigarette.

Access to Hebron is through the H1 sector, theoretically under Palestinian control. According to a protocol established last year, some eighty percent of the one hundred twenty-six thousand inhabitants of

168

Hebron live in H1 sector. The H2 sector, which covers a large portion of the old city, has a population of around forty thousand, including some four or five hundred Jewish settlers. The modern centre distinguishes itself with a few high rise buildings, mainly office space ; most are only half constructed. In the sunshine village people crowd the market. As we make our way through the old souk towards the Sanctuary of Abraham (Al-Haram AI-Ibrahimi) – Gerard and Pierrette are my travel companions today – we are shocked at the spectacle. Hebron has been killed. It is not so much the dilapidated state of the buildings and streets that strikes us ; there is plenty of evidence of recent, well-executed restoration work. It is the deathly silence, the row upon row of shuttered shops daubed with Stars of David ; the empty streets, watchtowers and video surveillance cameras ; the wire fencing and concrete bollards that have transformed lively thoroughfares into dead streets. Near the Sanctuary Jewish settlers have taken up residence in the upper floors of the ancient buildings. Most, we are told, come from France and the United States. They are protected by soldiers standing on every corner. It is a scene of hatred. A system of nets protects the Palestinian pedestrians from objects thrown by settlers from their upper floor flats. We make our way through narrow alleys and streets, walking under nets weighed down by assorted rubbish (rusted tins, empty bottles), hugging the walls. I raise my eyes to the upper floors and glimpse Israeli flags and windows with thick bars. They are recent additions, carried out with little respect for the historical character of the site. Hanging over a balcony, a young boy peppers passers-by with stones. An Israeli soldier – perhaps his older brother – reasons with him gently, but the stubborn little dolt persists, convinced of his rights. This one street, the only passageway to the mosque, is an assault course of humiliation. On the green shutters of a closed shop I read in Cyrillic letters smiert arabham (death to the Arabs) and on the shutters of the facing shop the authors of this graffiti reveal themselves, " Sacha, Youri ". A few steps further down someone has spray-painted more slogans, again in Russian, " Struggle without compromise ", " Fight to the death ". Thank goodness, not everyone who lives in the souk reads Russian.

Gerard and Pierrette can't get over the scene. " It makes your flesh creep. " A young man hails us and invites us into his house for coffee. The sitting room is a small square room ; two rib vaults support the ceiling. The walls are so thick, the openings so small, that the dwelling seems to be carved out of the rock. The young man introduces us to his father, Mohammed Taleeb, the sixty year-old patriarch of the family, he invites us to sit on the red sofas. The only book in view is a large green Qur'an. Embroidered Qur'anic verses and a tapestry representing Mecca hang on the walls. Everyday, the young man explains, the family reads a verse together. Gradually the room fills with women and children. The patriarch's wife – she has put on a white headscarf to greet us – takes her seat at his side. Daughters, daughters-in-law, children... Father and son are builders ; the father is invalid and no longer works. He mentions back pains. He introduces his family as each member enters the room. Twenty-two people live under his roof in six separate rooms distributed around a single staircase. His wife gave him six sons and seven daughters ;

170

nearly all are married now and parents of many children. The youngest enter the room and greet the visitors respectfully with a handshake or a triple kiss ; then they take their place on their parents' knees. They appear properly fed and dressed, surrounded by affection. They go to primary or secondary school, but university is too expensive. The latest addition to the family, an infant boy, passes from hand to hand with his infant smile. Orangeade is served, then candy and coffee. The daughters-in-law are the first to leave, respectfully kissing the hand and forehead of the patriarch, then the matriarch. She utters not a word – perhaps because she knows no English ? – smiling and sitting upright next to her husband, her brown, lightly wrinkled, statuesque face set off beautifully by the white triangle of her headscarf.

The Taleebs have developed their own modest form of resistance by sustaining life, bringing countless children into the world, cementing a family through tradition and religion. As we prepare to leave, the patriarch shows us a picture of a nephew, a Reuter's journalist recently killed in Baghdad. One more martyr.

In the centre of the old city, the Sanctuary of Abraham is stylistically diverse. Here, for over twenty centuries, worshipers have venerated their illustrious ancestors : Abraham, Sarah, Isaac, Rebecca, Jacob, Leah and Joseph. The remains are found in a cave located a few metres further down. The twenty-meter high walls around the sanctuary date from Herod. The crenellated upper part of the wall dates from Mamluk times. Crusaders added their own personal touch to the interior with clerestory windows over the main entrance and arched vaulting, which replaced the original flat ceiling. The famous carved wood minbar was made in the eleventh century. For over a century the sanctuary was Saint Abraham Cathedral, then it became a mosque (with the edification of two minarets and five cenotaphs). Today it is both a mosque (left entrance) and a synagogue (right entrance). On Friday February 24, 1994, Baruch Goldstein, a settler from Kiryat Arba, clad in military garb, stormed into the sanctuary and gunned down Muslim worshipers, killing twenty-nine, wounding two hundred. Since then access to the sanctuary is heavily policed. Worshipers and tourists must pass through electronic detectors and submit to body searches. Israeli soldiers ask visitors what religion they are. As good French citizens – and by no means wishing to engage in a discussion of metaphysical preferences with the military authorities, especially since they are armed to the teeth – we declare ourselves " without religion ". " What ? That doesn't exist ! " exclaims a female soldier. Are their instructions to refuse entry of Jews to the mosque and non-Jews to the synagogue ?

A partition separates the mosque and the synagogue ; worshipers on both sides of the shrine are audible to each other. It is even possible to see each other through the grating that opens onto Abraham's cenotaph. In theory nothing prevents Jewish and Muslim worshipers from seeing each other and speaking together from their respective sides of the small chapel. I suggest the following improbable essay topic for the young students of Hebron/Al-Khalil : " Abraham B. and Ibrahim A. greet each other through the grating of the sanctuary shared by their two religions. Imagine their conversation. "

172

There is a tourist facility for Jewish visitors outside the synagogue entrance. It includes a cafeteria, souvenir shop, stalls selling religious articles and public toilets marked with a large Star of David. Next to the facility are an Israeli police station and a bus stop serving the Kiryat Arba settlement, where Hebron settlers go shopping. Several vehicles with yellow number plates (Israelis) are parked out front. The Arab souvenir shops are closed ; they look as if they have been abandoned for a long time. Settlers come and go ; lots of men with kippahs and locks. Two young pregnant women, wearing long dresses and bell hats, stroll along, each surrounded by three children.

The first street to the left reminds me of a movie plot seen a hundred times : the survivor of a nuclear or chemical holocaust wanders alone through the empty streets of a town ; buildings are still intact, but all life has disappeared.

A child appears at a balcony ; another ventures into the street below. The one on the balcony grabs a broom and sweeps an empty bottle onto the street. He misses his target. The two children vanish and silence resumes. The afternoon sun casts lacy shadows onto the walls.

Some soldiers are standing at the end of the street. I strike up a conversation with a jovial looking one. He is from Brazil.

" What are you doing here ? " he asks.

– What about you ? I reply.

– Maintaining order.

– Order or disorder ?

– Order of the disorder, if you prefer. In the 1920s sixty Jews were killed here ; we have to protect the Jewish presence in Hebron.
– Fifteen hundred soldiers to protect five hundred settlers. Is that normal in your opinion ? – Normal or not normal, what difference does it make ? Any way, I'm just following army orders.
– Well, if you want my opinion, you'd be better off leaving the army.
– Then what would I do ? How would I make a living ? "

Brecht would have loved this soldier. I try to imagine Brecht wandering the streets of Hebron at nightfall. No doubt he would strike up a conversation with the two pregnant settlers. Who are they ? How do they live ? What are their personal dreams ? Their dreams for their children ? I can't muster the courage to engage in conversation with them.

Distinguishing between civilians and soldiers seems rather pointless here. There are men, women and children on the Israeli frontline who are ready to kill and die in order to establish Jewish rights in Hebron, and beyond in the " Great Israel ". The army claims to protect them. No doubt it uses them. More seasoned than the soldiers themselves, the settlers are doubly armed civilians.*.

Twenty or so children run towards the mosque for soup with coloured plastic buckets. Further along, in an alleyway of the souk, an olive-skinned eleven year-old fights with an even more ragged-looking boy. The dark-complexioned one aims his punches with

---

* In the tally of Israeli deaths during the Intifada (between September 2000 and February 2006), the military accounted for 31%, civilian settlers for 23% (source : B'Tselem).

precision ; the other ducks and weaves helplessly. No shouts, no cries ; they fight like men. An adult in a bulky cardigan comes out of a café to separate them, but as soon as he turns his back, the fight resumes. The weaker one finally runs away.

Six young soldiers dash down the main artery of the old city bent on dispersing passers-by and closing down the few shops that are still open. Eyes stuck to the sights of their M16s, they aim their weapons in every direction like video game characters. The street empties instantaneously. A child hides in the folds of his mother's coat. A forty-year-old man with a black and white checked keffiyeh advances cautiously, raising his jacket to bare his stomach (to show he is not wearing an explosive belt). Scenes of an ordinary day in sector H2. " They announce a curfew when it suits them, at anytime of day or night " says an old shopkeeper. " It's impossible to make a living here. Those who can afford it get out of this place and start a business in H1.»

From time to time we come across young Europeans – Norwegians, Danes and Italians – wearing red armbands with the letters TIPH (Temporary International Presence in Hebron), sometimes on foot, sometimes in Land Rovers. They are here, they explain, " to observe the implementation of the 1997 agreements and keep a daily register of incidents. Not to intervene. " They are not international volunteers but civil servants paid by their respective governments. We later learn that their headquarters, located on the surrounding heights at a distance, is the only place we have any chance of buying alcohol.

At the Hebron-France Cultural Centre, located across from the university, we are welcomed by a half dozen students in different departments (technology, pharmacy...) and two teachers. A round of introductions. When they realise that Gerard is a philosopher they initiate a discussion on the topic of suicide. Their question is : " How do you qualify a military operation, in which a combatant sacrifices his life to kill the enemy ? Doesn't the word suicide create confusion, suggesting psychological motivations of a personal nature ? " In no hurry to reply, Gerard invites them to give their own opinions on the issue. Their approval of these " operations " – as they are called here – is not surprising. In turn, they answer our questions and tell us about their student lives. Because the army keeps the university closed most of the time, classes take place in a primary school in the afternoon after the children have gone home. They try to help one another and learn French at the cultural centre in the hope of obtaining a scholarship one day. The conversation takes place over tea between polite adults. They are well dressed and speak French haltingly but comprehensibly, with poised voices. Are they really prepared to die ? Or are they preoccupied with their personal and professional futures ? Perhaps inextricably with both ? Since the early days of suicide attacks – I will continue to use the term for lack of a better expression – Palestinian universities (especially Nablus and Hebron) have provided many candidates : serious young people, no doubt like the ones seated around the table. Clearly the students here identify with the suicide candidates. As we talk, we learn that a Palestinian has killed himself near Tel Aviv. " At least four dead " one of the students announces soberly.

Are they pleased ? Pierrette sees a student watching television in the next room break into a smile. But there are no shouts of joy, not now in the Hebron-France Cultural Centre, not later that evening in the restaurants and cafés. Every attack is followed by a curfew of unpredictable length, imposed more or less rigorously, depending on the origin of the suicide bomber. Three hours later the army closes down the sector and demolishes the suicide bomber's family house.

The next day Haaretz runs a story on Shehad Hanani, the 21 year-old suicide bomber who detonated himself at the Geha bus station. He was from Beit Furik near Nablus, one of the most harshly cordoned villages. In the paper's next issue, the correspondent Gideon Levy reports that the Israeli military killed Shehad's brother, Fadi Hanani, ten days earlier in Nablus.

The evening is spent in the company of a young Palestinian intellectual who speaks his mind freely and boldly. Zyad studied history and archaeology ; he is also interested in philosophy. He drills us on the headscarf ban in French schools ; the topic comes around frequently in conversations here, not least since Islamist movements organise frequent protest rallies. Zyad detects an expression of anti-Muslim sentiment in the ban, which he believes is spreading throughout French society because of a lack of understanding of the religious phenomenon itself. In the same frame of thought, he registers surprise at French legislation against religious sects, among the harshest anywhere in Europe. He doesn't consider himself religious at all. " Here, religion is absolute hypocrisy. Everything is taboo. Everything is forbidden, so everything is done in hiding, including homosexual acts. God forbid we should mention them ! Did you see the movie Kaddosh by the Israeli Amos Gitai ? It's the same thing here. Love is taboo. " In politics as well, Zyad's positions are anything but orthodox. " Palestinians are told they descend from the Canaanites and Israelis from the Hebrews. That's idiotic brainwashing. School children should learn that Palestine has always been the dustbin of the Middle East and that people of all origins can be found here. We don't need a Palestinian state anymore than we need a Jewish state. What we need is a Middle East without state borders. The United States cannot possibly offer a solution to the needs of the people today. " By the end of the evening, when we return to the issue of suicide bombings, Zyad is unambiguous in his condemnation : " The imams are brainwashing our youth. "

December 26th. The early morning bus to Hebron-Bethlehem leaves the station on time but soon has to turn around and head back. Soldiers block the road and wave their weapons threateningly. Our foreign passports allow us to continue our journey and we hitch a ride to Jerusalem. But our fellow bus passengers will either abandon their travel plans or use the many off-road solutions to reach their respective destinations.

The same day we have an invitation to visit the Shtayah family home in Kufar Naameh, a small village west of Ramallah. A lovely new house high up the hill ; the view is fantastic. The sky is clear ; the sea vaguely visible in the distance. The mistress of the house and her three daughters – one a university student, the other two in high school – have prepared a banquet for some twenty guests. Musakhan (an oven-baked flat bread served with onions and chicken marinated in spices) and makloube (an upside down casserole of rice and braised lamb), both Palestinian national dishes. They are accompanied with the usual condiments, yoghurt, olives, sweet and dill pickles, peppers and black radishes marinated in vinegar. Everyone drinks lemonade and coca cola with the meal. After the lovely food, the conversation turns once again to the headscarf ban in France, a topic that stirs even the ire of the Shtayak family, which is hardly observant. The law is seen as a form of anti-Muslim persecution, an attempt on the part of the French to wriggle back into the good graces of the White House. Arab TV networks have given such extensive coverage to the issue that our hosts conclude that all women regardless of age will be forbidden to wear a headscarf in public places in France.

With some effort we bring the conversation back to Palestine and this particular village. Kufar Naameh, a farming community of some three thousand souls, depends for its livelihood on the olives and figs sold by its coop. Fifteen hundred children attend the village's two schools (which places the village within the national statistical average, since fifty-three percent of Palestinians are under the age of seventeen). The village has three mosques ; two appear almost new. Nayef Shtayah teaches mathematics and science at the elementary school ; he is also secretary to the mayor. He boasts the inauguration of a village library, two leisure centres, a kindergarten and a " democratic club for women and children ". Five years ago the village built a water tower but wasn't able to use it ; the army seized it almost immediately and transformed it into a

179

watchtower ; it simultaneously took control of the village's water distribution. A detachment of soldiers now permanently occupies a rocky outcrop at the base of the tower, an excellent promontory from which they can survey all traffic, villages and Jewish settlements in the sector. Because water cuts are frequent, local villagers have started to dig wells again and collect rainwater. Most are supporters of Fatah, but Hamas and Islamic Jihad have their backers too. Nayef Shtayah is not keen to elaborate on the topic. A black flag waves on a neighbouring house. " That's Riad Khalifa's house. He was killed ten days ago. Thirty-three years old. He was a fatherless orphan ; married only three months. If you are interested, after lunch we can visit his mother. He escaped from prison and the Israeli authorities were looking for him. They killed him nearby. He was a member of Islamic Jihad. "

A poor house at the end of a dirt road. A cement floor, bare walls, plastic chairs set against the walls for visitors paying their respects. The mother is a tough old peasant woman with large calloused hands, ruddy cheeks, dressed entirely in black. For the hundredth time she tells the story of the last time she saw her son ; the last meal she prepared for him. It was a Thursday ; he died on a Sunday. Ten or so neighbours listen to the story they already know by heart. No one asks questions. No one mentions the informer who probably tipped off the army as to Riad's whereabouts. The grandmother, a tiny woman with a weather-beaten, heavily wrinkled face, comes into the room. Sits down without a word. The shahid's widow is seated next to her mother-in-law. All of eighteen years old ; the face of a child, completely wrapped in silence. Blue jeans under her large black veil. Three generations of mourning women in this room ; woe, woe and woe again. My pity goes out to the youngest of the three : only recently married to – forced to wed ? – a man much older than her ; a fighter, a prisoner on the run. Word has it she is pregnant. Has she known happiness ? What fate awaits her ? Will she now have to live under the iron rule of her mother-in-law ? Will she be allowed to remarry ? In the circumstances of the mourning ritual one can only listen to the platitudes and keep quiet.

Later in the afternoon a young man from the village fills me in. " Every time Riad saw an Israeli he would say I'm going to get that one, I'm going to kill him. He never finished school. He was sixteen when he went to prison for the first time. He spent ten years there ; his final years were spent in hiding. He was a very good shot, but a hot head. As we carried him to his grave, we heard his wife was pregnant ; we told him as we laid him to rest and covered him with earth. "

A fighter from the youngest age, an armed resistant, didn't Riad choose his own fate – to a degree anyway ? Why does the village weep over him like a victim rather than a hero ? Why does the same word shahid apply indifferently to everyone ? These are questions I have asked my Palestinian friends repeatedly, but I have never received a satisfying answer.

I realise I have used the word " pity " here. It makes me uncomfortable.

Nablus has been under siege since December 26th. The army occupied the city after the attack in Petah Tikva, which resulted in four dead and twelve wounded. Eager to put the events on film and laden with heavy camera equipment, Robin and Jean-Philippe leave at the end of the morning for Nablus. They give me a call around two in the afternoon : " It's war here. Tanks everywhere. Kids are throwing rocks and soldiers are firing back with live ammunition. " So much for my neighbour Mussa's wedding engagement celebration and for the New Year's Eve party we had planned. I grab my things and leave immediately. I stash two bottles of alcohol in my rucksack, in case we have to spend New Year's Eve under curfew ; I add a book (Proust, The Prisoner), in case things go wrong.

Good news : since the removal of the Surda checkpoint, the bus runs a regular service again. Departure time 2.30 p.m. ; the ticket is affordable (ten shekels) ; the route more direct than in November. The bus is packed. Crowded together at the back, a few children voice their excitement at the journey. The road winds through olive groves and passes close to settlements visible in the distance.

An hour later I arrive at the Hawara checkpoint. When the duty soldier sees my foreign passport and press card, he alerts his commanding officer. Outright refusal. I point out that my two colleagues crossed the same checkpoint this morning. " Nablus is closed to everyone, including journalists. Your colleagues didn't come through here. Impossible. They must have sneaked through the mountains. It's closed here. Do you understand ? We have orders. This isn't Parliament ; you don't discuss orders here. If you don't like it, call the army spokesperson. " The checkpoint's Cerberus has the physique for the job : a blond mop protruding from his helmet ; heavy build ; a fat belly which his body armour accents ; blood-shot eyes ; skin blotches and a puffy nose. On the army switchboard I talk to a person who hands me over to a second then a third. The line goes dead. Half an hour goes by. Two Israeli women volunteers from Macksom Watch scribble in their notepads. I ask for their help, on the off chance. They are not here to intervene, they say with a friendly smile ; their role is to observe how human rights are respected. Much later, after night falls and they are ready to leave, they will give me their last croissant.

A Land Rover arrives ; it appears to belong to a media organisation. The driver agrees to help me pass through the checkpoint and offers me a seat in front. We coast ten meters to the barrier. This time the hellhound erupts in anger, orders me out of the vehicle and confiscates my passport and press card. " You countermanded my orders ! You tried to sneak through behind my back ! This is very serious ! I am

184

going to inform the high command. " The driver of the Land Rover, more than happy to have authorisation to proceed, waves at me in sympathy and disappears. I resume my wait behind the barrier with the two humanitarian observers.

A wrinkled woman in rags, so tiny she is almost a dwarf, begs the soldier in charge. She has been here for hours, night is falling, she has nowhere to go, no money, she can't turn back. With piercing shrieks she attempts to arouse the sympathy of the others waiting to cross. An old man defends her case. Wasted effort.

As for me, without a passport, I'm stuck here too ; all I can do is call the Consulate. I manage to reach a competent civil servant on the phone, a minor miracle on New Year's Eve. He expresses concern ; will try to find out more ; insists I call him back if the situation changes. I wait another half hour, gradually putting on all the warm clothes I had taken precaution to throw into my small rucksack.

A few metres away a young man is helped to his feet. I hadn't noticed him before ; he was concealed from view behind two concrete blocks. He is blindfolded, arms bound behind his back. He is skinny and appears weak, freezing cold. His only clothes are a torn shirt and jeans. He leans on the arm of another, older Palestinian in a green anorak. He takes the young man ten metres away, next to a parked car, and helps him with a difficult task. The prisoner tries to spread his legs, manages to urinate ; his companion holds him on his feet, almost carries him, then brings him back to the two concrete blocks where he collapses.

I ask the two observers about him. " He's been here since this morning ". – What did he do ? – Nobody knows. "

I go back to the soldiers. A small dark-skinned one with the face of a child says a few kind words in French. His mother is from France ; he was born in Israel ; it doesn't seem to please him that much. " You're not afraid of trouble if the duty officer sees you talking with me ? – Not really. He yells a lot. It's no big deal. " The other soldier – thickset, almost fat, blond with light blue eyes – comes over and joins us. As soon as he hears I speak Russian, he relaxes and is almost friendly. His nick name is Micha. " The prisoner ? He didn't do anything. We're after his brother. – And why are you here ? Are you doing your military service ? – Not at all. I finished three years. But I signed up for five more years. I have two to go. – Why did you volunteer for the army ? – To serve my country. Already when I was in Russia I wanted to be a soldier. I was born in Moscow, then emigrated to Canada with my parents. Now I'm here. – Did you have strong religious beliefs ? – At first, yes. I tried to be observant, but the army spoils you. I'm not religious anymore. – And the officer there ? Is he in charge here ? – No, the young guy there, he's the commanding officer. "

I address the young commanding officer in English, a tall skinny boy with freckles ; he floats in his uniform, a clever bookish type. " Do you plan on keeping my passport a long time ? You know it's illegal to confiscate my I.D. ? If I broke a law without knowing, just give me a fine. – I know the law better than you. And I know what kind of person you are. You hate us. – I beg your pardon ? – You hate Jews.

186

You journalists are all the same. " He walks away in a hurry, fearing he has said too much.

As for Micha, he's more the talkative kind. " So you've been to Russia ? " – A few times. I had cousins in Leningrad. They live in California now. – And what are you doing here ? – I'm writing. – A novel ? – Something like that. Your commanding officer there would make a good character in a novel. He's the first person here to call me anti-Semitic. – Well, it's true, everyone is against us. In Canada too. – Really ? How is that ? – Every time I leave Canada for Israel I see how they look at my passport at the airport. They don't like it. – It looks like your commanding officer is talking about me on the phone over there. – That's right. We'll probably let you go through. Not right away, but in fifteen or twenty minutes. He's talking with Headquarters now. But, really, why do you want to go to Nablus ? – To see what's happening and to meet up with some friends. – And where will you spend the night ? – In a hotel. – You mean there are hotels in Nablus ? – Of course, what do you think ? – I don't know. I've never been there. "

As we talk, night falls and the temperature drops a few more degrees. I have had plenty of time to contemplate the wooded heights in the distance ; the barbed wire and piles of rubbish at my feet ; the guard posts and watchtowers further down the slope. Two shebab arrive carrying a sports bag. A soldier searches the bag and finds a small tapestry illustrating a pair of handcuffed arms reaching to the sky. Probably the symbol of a resistance group ; something is written in Arabic that the soldier cannot decipher. He asks a colleague to help. The incident drags on. The contents of the bag are scattered on the ground and the soldier cautiously sifts through items of clothing with the barrel of his weapon.

A small car arrives for the two female observers. At the same moment an armoured van stops at the barrier ; the prisoner, still blindfolded and handcuffed, is forced into the back ; he collapses to the floor, a metallic sound echoes with his fall. The Israeli car (yellow number plates) and van disappear into the distance, one towards Tel Aviv, the other in the direction of a military interrogation centre.

There aren't many people left in the queue. A young manager-type in reefer jacket carrying an attaché case pleads his case, first in Arabic, then in English. " Can you interpret " asks Micha ? We don't understand a word he's saying. – He says he lives just on the other side ; he'd like to go home ; his family is waiting for him. – Tell him to see the commanding officer. "

I ask myself what I'm doing here in the middle of the West Bank, on New Year's Eve, interpreting for the Israeli army, especially since they have confiscated my I.D. Another car arrives driven by a young man ; it has three veiled passengers. Much gesturing. The driver points to an old woman in the front seat, who appears semi-conscious. Micha remarks, " He says she's bleeding, but how do we know he isn't lying. They always try to trick us. – Well, in their shoes, do you think you'd tell the truth ? – In their shoes ? ! " The question makes Micha wonder, as if the thought had never crossed his mind.

The old woman is helped from the car. She wobbles. She is allowed across on foot, but the rest of the family must turn around. Another fifteen minutes before an ambulance from the other side arrives to fetch her.

After three or four long telephone conversations, one with the French Consulate, the fat red-faced officer hands me back my documents and invites me politely to cross the barrier. " Sorry for the inconvenience, Madam ", he says with a deferential smile that was not there earlier, " I'm really very sorry. "

What has caused this turnabout ? Is it the Consul's doing ? Have they finally understood I'm Jewish too ? I pass through quickly with no idea of what awaits me on the other side. I phone the consulate to thank them for their assistance and to wish them a Happy New Year. " Call us if you have a problem. We're not comfortable knowing you're in Nablus right now. But we managed to convince the army that a woman your age was safer in a hotel in Nablus than on the road, isn't that right ? – In short, my age made the difference ? – Ah, no, we, ah your age…it's your business, isn't it ? – Thanks again. "

I haven't gone a hundred metres when the officer shouts imperiously, " Come back ! Come back ! " There is no hesitating. I'm not going to run the risk of being shot. So it's back to the checkpoint again. " You can't get into Nablus at this time of night without a vehicle. Nobody walks the streets. Wait here. " A car is requisitioned ; it belongs to a Palestinian doctor who has been waiting at the checkpoint for an hour or more. He looks fifty ; an upright citizen, suit, tie, white shirt. Maybe he is being allowed through on condition that he chauffeurs me into town ? The fact that the army is offering me its protection puts neither of us at ease. As we enter the city there is not a car, not a pedestrian in the streets.

Piles of smoking rubble block the passageway here and there; we are forced to zigzag our way through, frequently driving onto the shoulder of the road. The doctor points to a blood stain in the street visible through the headlights of his car. " I can't take you any further. It's too dangerous. – Don't take any risks for me. I know your family is waiting for you. " We see a taxi coming in the opposite direction; it refuses to take me into the city centre. Two ambulance drivers accept to give me a lift. In the back I have a choice between a gurney and a seat. I choose the seat and we set off down the street in a totally blacked-out city; not a street lamp shines in the streets, not a light in the windows. Flames flicker in overturned rubbish bins. Stones, rubble and debris are scattered across the road, suggesting the violence of the confrontation that appears to have ended only moments earlier. A tank blocks the road in front of us; the ambulance turns left. Another tank further along; the ambulance turns down the first narrow alley. Armoured vans drive by just behind us. The ambulance comes to a stop at the foot of some steps. " Here you are. Good luck. " I offer to pay for the ride. My Saint Bernard rescuers refuse any suggestion of money, then disappear into the night.

I climb the steps to Hotel Yasmeen like a lone survivor struggling to shore after a shipwreck. It is not yet seven p.m.. My friends from the production team greet me, as do the hotel receptionist, an interpreter-guide and a few foreign visitors. More or less all have been following my adventure through the Hawara checkpoint. They have been locked in the hotel since

190

the beginning of the afternoon, when the street fighting really turned violent. I must admit, if I think about it and examine the concerns of the Israeli defence forces, I was probably held back at the barrier until the situation in the city centre quieted down. Everyone in Palestine knows that the Intifada has its time schedule. The hottest moment, when the shebab are out throwing rocks in greatest numbers, is always in the middle of the afternoon. It usually cools down when night falls. Of course the unexpected arrival of a column of armoured vehicles in a town or village can upset this time table, but on the whole... In other words, seven p.m. was about the right time for me to arrive.

The reception area on the first floor looks onto the tiny street, through which I have just arrived, on the one side and faces Al-Nasr Mosque and the bell tower in the middle of the kasbah on the other.

We strike up a conversation with three Italians of my generation (twenty year olds back in 1968) and a much younger group of people from Sweden, Norway, Belgium, Germany, England, and France. Let's have a drink; after all it's New Year's Eve. We're in luck; the hotel serves wine (inconceivable in Hebron or Gaza). Suddenly, two huge explosions. They sound very near. Those with practiced ears hazard a guess : " The Israelis are demolishing houses in the Old City. "

Quiet returns after a quarter of an hour. Then we hear appeals in Arabic over a loudspeaker : " The unified command of Nablus resistance calls residents to climb on to the terraces and shout " Allah is great ", translates Farid, the hotel's young interpreter-guide. All the young people at the international table stand and prepare to venture out on a reconnaissance mission. We follow in their footsteps in single file and exit the hotel by a staircase at the back, which spills directly into a narrow alley of the souk. It's totally dark. An Israeli tank is posted at an intersection a hundred metres away. With hands in the air, we shout again and again : " We are internationals. We are here to see if there are any wounded and help the rescuers with evacuation. " Go away ! Fuck you ! says a voice in a megaphone. We cut into another alley. Another tank. Go away ! Our little procession is led by Mika, a young British Jew, who knows the kasbah well and speaks some Arabic. He has been living with a small team of volunteers in Balata refugee camp for about four months now. Sporting a blonde goatee, his skinny silhouette floats in an over-sized anorak ; his gait is limber and quick, his stare concentrated, as he picks his way through the narrow streets knowingly. We are now making our way down one of the main arteries of the souk, sidestepping rubbish and broken glass. Many windows are broken. Residents stand at their windows, shouting encouragements. Forget the idea that they might come down and join us ; most haven't left their flats for four or five days. We run into several Medical Relief ambulances. Each one is operated by two young rescuers who wear red reflector jackets.

Another tank, another Go away ! We approach some Israeli soldiers who seem relaxed. They are very young, probably upset that they have to spend New Year's Eve in an armoured van in the middle of a city with a bad reputation for danger. One of the young internationals says, " Their eyes look wild ; they're probably high and drunk. " They begin to talk

192

together, slurring their speech and ignoring the camera and microphone. A young woman hails us from a window above ; an old grandmother up there is not well. The ambulance volunteers go have a look. Nothing serious ; no need to take her to hospital emergency. Nearby, a large gate has been smashed open, probably by a tank. Strangely, a few cars are still parked untouched ; neither crushed nor burned. The ambulance personnel tell us they have taken many wounded shebab to hospital today, but no dead.

Someone looks at his watch. It's nearly midnight. Our group stops in the middle of an intersection. Two young activists from Lille join our group, then a Greek, then a Norwegian finishing his linguistics studies here. There must be ten or more ambulance personnel standing around with us too. A resident brings down a thermos. The three Italians launch into a rendition of Bella ciao. They sing every verse, including partigiano morto per la libertà, which brings tears to our eyes. I sing a few lines of The International (what else in such company ?). While the astonished ambulance drivers look on, the Italians – Donatella from Bergamo and Barbara from Milan – join me in the refrain " 'Tis the final conflict ".

Thursday morning. Confirmation that, indeed, the Abdel-Hadi Castle was attacked by mortar and dynamite. Dating from the Eighteenth century this three-storey building was home to sixteen families. A few days later the Office for the Coordination of Humanitarian Affairs (OCHA) announces its assessment of the attack : three houses in the old city completely destroyed ; thirty-five rendered uninhabitable ; ten heavily damaged and several dozen have had their windows blown out.

This morning the production team has grown : Robin on camera, Jean-Philippe on sound, Farid as interpreter-guide and me. We pace up and down the souk's empty alleys. Despite the curfew a few shops raise their shutters in order to enable families to buy essentials. Impossible to get anywhere close to the castle ; all access points are blocked by tanks.

Farid knocks at the door of the Khammash family, friends whose terrace overlooks the castle. The door is opened by a slender man with an unkempt grey beard ; he is still in pyjamas. A beautiful, shapely woman, eyes puffy with sleep, is making coffee. " Please come in. No bother at all ! " say Samir and Hanane in unison. The flat has two large square rooms with high vaulted ceilings. They have been restored recently and tastefully. No religious ornaments whatsoever. Samir is a painter and sculptor but earns his living as superintendent at the Hotel Yasmeen. Hanane raises their six children : three boys and three girls. There is also a little dog, which never leaves Samir's lap. Quickly, the mattresses in the living room are tucked away and the sofas put back in place for the guests. Only the youngest child (five years old) lies in bed, sucking his thumb under the covers. Muhammad (twelve years old) hasn't been to school for a week. The other children are nowhere to be seen this morning.

In front of the camera Samir talks about everyday life in Nablus over the past few days ; the army forcibly removing families from their flats in order to fortify its positions ; the sick without access to care ; children no longer able to go to school ; little ones suffering from nightmares. " Food and supplies ? We get by. The shopkeepers go door-to-door.

Money ? Families help each other out ; we borrow if necessary. " Sometimes the family dog yaps during the interview. Leaning against the door, Muhammad listens to his father's answers. " Does Muhammad throw rocks ? – Of course, like all boys his age. – That doesn't frighten you ? – What difference does it make ? He's putting up resistance, doing what he can, like all of us. – Don't you think he would be more useful to the resistance if he finishes his education ? – Maybe, but we can't stop him from going out with the others. " Hanane winces ; she clearly disagrees with her husband. We encourage her to speak out. " Perhaps a mother can sacrifice her son, if it is worthwhile. But not like this ! This violence is so senseless ! It's leading us nowhere. " Samir does not contradict her. She expresses herself more freely than he does, with less concern for " political correctness ". Off camera I pursue the conversation with Samir. " Why did people go up onto the roofs last evening and shout 'Allah is great' rather than 'Free Palestine' ? – Because they are waging war against Muslims ! – Oh ? I thought Israelis were fighting Palestinians, not Muslims ? – What about Iraq ? Afghanistan ? Bush and Sharon are exactly the same ! "

Samir and his son take us out onto the terrace. We can see the neighbour's flat ; it has been entirely demolished, two floors collapsed on top of each other. " The army dynamited the place last year. It's my cousin's. " Most of the Khammash cousins live in the same block of houses. The castle is in the opposite direction, totally surrounded by tanks. We can't appreciate last night's destruction from here. The pale sunlight of the New Year begins to spill over us and onto the interconnecting terraces of the kasbah.

Hanane brings up a tray of orangeade drinks. What can I wish for the New Year ?

In the ensuing days the media make a tally of the fighting : five armed men, sixteen unarmed men, including six under the age of eighteen, killed in Nablus by the Israeli army between December 16 and January 7. The correspondent for the Guardian mentions two cold-blooded executions, victims " shot at close range, bodies like sieves, horrible slashes, dog bites ". The Israeli army promises to open an inquest.

3 – 14 January

Under sunny skies I go out for a walk with Marie, a friend who arrived from Paris yesterday. We pass beside the Iron Curtain behind the Grand Park Hotel near the cement factory. In the distance the workers wave a greeting. On the return portion of our walk they make room for us in their van and drive us back to the centre of Ramallah. We head for the Muqataa and stop in the courtyard. " If you like, I can take a picture of you both ", says a young soldier in jeans. Here we are, standing and smiling in front of what was once a Palestinian guard post ; it has been entirely destroyed. The atmosphere is friendly. Only one restriction : " Please don't film the faces of the security personnel. " We are admitted into the courtyard without any control ; Marie can't believe it. The heap of burnt out cars, surmounted by a Palestinian flag, is as photogenic as ever. One of the security guards spent a year of military training in Beijing. Marie says a few words in Chinese to him ; they burst out laughing. The soldiers offer us coffee but make another request, " Please don't make too much noise, Abu Amar is taking a nap ".

4–5 January. An international conference against the occupation is being held in East Jerusalem. Ilan Pappe, the Israeli historian, speaks about the nakba (the 1948 Palestinian catastrophe) and " Zionist foundations of ethnic cleansing ". The official term in use at the time was " purification ", the same word used in the burning of leavened bread on the eve of Passover. This demand for a state " purified " of its Arab elements, the historian underlines, does not emanate from the religious right, but from the secular left and the trade union movement.

7 January. Early in the morning we leave for Gaza, with no guarantee that we will be admitted. We have the backing of the French Consulate which sent a fax to Israeli authorities confirming we are expected at the French Cultural Centre in Gaza City. Today, by special taxi, the crossing from Kalandia to Erez will take us less than two hours, despite the rush hour traffic around Jerusalem. We arrive at 9.15. A real border post with a large garrison. Erez is nothing like the checkpoints in the West Bank. Foreign visitors, VIPs and journalists, pass through a prefabricated building, well lighted, heated, furnished with chairs and a drinks distributor. As for Palestinians, they are sent down a separate passageway ; we see it in the distance, empty, with no amenities whatsoever. It opens on to a vast parking area designed for dozens of buses. Empty at this time of the morning.

On the VIP side, soldiers are relatively polite, not at all under stress. In-coming and out-going traffic is very limited. Sergeant Blumberg (his name is on his uniform), a big dark-haired thirty year-old, invokes a new security measure in effect since January 1st ; he refuses passage to Marie. We wait patiently for two hours ; call the army spokesperson ; ask the Consulate to intervene again. A stroke of luck, the Consul in person appears. He is in a hurry, rather embarrassed. He repeats : we did everything necessary ; naturally it's not up to us to decide, but to " our Israeli friends ". Red Cross and UNO employees, diplomats, a few foreign journalists...a Chinese journalist, pulling a big suitcase on wheels, leave Gaza. Four or five Palestinians with special status pass through the office. When all goes well the wait is usually twenty minutes. " Worse than a prison gate ", my friend comments. At eleven o'clock, the refusal is final. We turn around and cross over the empty square. Back to Israel. On the highway to Ashkelon we hitch a ride with a lorry driver ; he drops us at a bus stop. Wind and rain. A dozen young people in uniform, huddle under the shelter, lots of girls with machine guns on their shoulders. Perfect target for an attack, we both think. Change of bus, more waiting with another group, exposed to the elements. Soldiers appear to be the main users of public transport in this country. They travel for free.

Full body search at the Jerusalem bus station. In Hebrew the word for security is bitakhon*. The word makes me laugh stupidly ; it's nervous laughter. In the washrooms, female soldiers stand in front of the mirrors and preen themselves to look good in their uniforms. Their generous backsides stretch the bottoms of their green trousers.

The crowded bus runs along Jaffa Street before reaching the old town. Everybody stares at each other, scared to death. Lots of kippahs, wigs, head wear and

---

* To a French ear bitakhon sounds like two words "bite" (prick) and "con" (pussy). (Trans. note)

coverings of all sorts. Men dressed in black and wearing wide-brimmed hats walk, prayer books in hand. A very fat Jewish woman takes a seat next to us. Her transparent plastic rain cap, worn over a black wig, is dripping wet. She has three large bags of wool balls ; she and her bags take up two of the three seats. We are squeezed against the steamed up window. What is she doing with so much wool ? Does she knit for the entire Jewish community ? The bus fills up with rain-drenched people loaded with bundles ; they look exhausted. The Russian women are immediately recognisable : post-Soviet style of clothing, hair dyed blonde or red, bright eyes and high cheeks. A chubby young woman decides to sit down and take the bags on her knees. We squeeze together a little closer to the window. When it finally reaches the old city, the bus empties completely.

8 January. We reach Qalqiliya at around eleven a.m.. It is entirely surrounded by the wall. Standing at the foot of the eight metre-high wall − grey slabs of concrete as far as the eye can see − we feel extremely small. Multi-coloured graffiti in many languages : This Wall will fall, Somos todos palestinos, Free Palestine. Soldiers aim their weapons at us from the watch tower, a grey cylinder perched on top the grey wall. We walk along the base of the wall under the watchful eye of surveillance cameras installed every twenty-five metres. It is raining. We trudge through ruts formed by heavy construction equipment. We walk past greenhouses where fruits and vegetable are still cultivated barely five metres from the wall. Beyond the greenhouses begins a street lined with cute new villas ; once their balconies had an unrestricted view over the countryside that stretches into the distance. Now

nothing is visible on the Jewish side from an Arab building.

The town of Qalqiliya is dying. It has lost the Israeli clientele that came every weekend to buy fruits and vegetables, to have their cars repaired, eat in inexpensive restaurants, have teeth looked after. Several thousand residents have also moved away. An unusual sight for a Thursday midday, rows of closed retail businesses and workshops line the empty streets. A shop sign displays a large molar tooth. We come across a delegation of foreign visitors under their umbrellas tramping along the wall behind a municipal official. Qalqiliya has become a pilgrimage for militant visitors. Marie is coughing harder and harder. The chemist sells cough syrup ; he also offers tea. We talk for a short while.

The Qalqiliya – Tulkarm " service " drives alongside the building site of the Iron Curtain on crudely paved roads for ten kilometres or so. The hills here are much greener than around Ramallah or Bethlehem. Stuck between the Green Line (pre-1967 border) and the Wall, explains a fellow passenger, the Arab villages are dying out here.

This forty year-old mountain of a man, so tall his head constantly bumps the roof of the Mercedes, suggests a practical solution to make our way to Jenin. His wife and children will be leaving in thirty minutes ; the taxi is already reserved. He takes us to his house. It's a single level house that looks a bit knocked together ; it opens onto an orchard of orange and lemon trees. The mother, Ulfa, is an English teacher, making conversation easier. Lively, affable, inquisitive, very modern in appearance, wearing a jogging suit with an American logo. Three children. The eldest, nineteen years old, built on the same imposing model as his father. (He won't be making the trip to see his cousins in Jenin because he has a mathematics exam Saturday morning.) A young, fifteen year-old girl, thin, long black hair, large dark eyes. The youngest, eleven, puny. " His best friend was killed before his eyes last year on the way to school ", his mother explains. " Since then he's been having nightmares ", the father adds, " and constantly asks to sleep in our bed ". Khaled sells and repairs computers. There are no religious symbols on the living room walls, but the interior offers various expressions of patriotism. Ulfa opens a curtain and shows us a picture of Khaled shaking Arafat's hand. " We keep it hidden ; if the soldiers see it, they will smash everything. " Another picture, in full view on a pedestal table, shows Arafat kissing the youngest son's hand. In the boys' bedroom there are ten copies of a shahid poster. " My husband's cousin, killed last year ", Ulfa explains. A picture of the shahid brandishing a kalachnikov is copied on the young girl's tee-shirt and on a medallion the youngest boy wears around his neck. Ulfa turns up the small fire, so we can dry our feet. (One of my socks is hung too close and goes up in smoke.) She brings tea, coffee, candy. Invites us to share her husband's lunch, rice and lamb. Thank you. We ate in Qalqiliya. The children show us around the house. " Last year a tank backed into the wall of my bedroom and demolished it completely, the young girl explains. When we rebuilt it, we took the opportunity to make it a little bigger ". Pictures of singers cover the walls ; there is another poster of the shahid cousin.

It's time to leave. Before going outside, Ulfa puts on a hijab and exchanges her jogging suit for a long jean dress that she covers with a long coat. Her daughter also covers her head. A sister-in-law and niece join us to take advantage of the long-distance taxi. Occasions to travel are rare. Ulfa hasn't seen her family for two years. " You will see ; our family in Jenin, the Rashid family, is extensive. "

It rains throughout the entire trip from Tulkarm to Jenin, which lasts about an hour. The countryside is lush and fertile, orchards and greenhouses everywhere. In the front seat the children hold gifts on their laps for the family and a bag of sugar for a wounded person. Ulfa talks about her youngest son who causes her worries ; then her family in Tulkarm and Jenin and the long months of siege that everyone has endured. As we enter Jenin, a pleasant surprise ; the checkpoint has been removed, momentarily anyway. She points to a building on the right where her brother lives. She will stay with him ; her children will stay with her sister on the other side of town. Ulfa insists : " Please, call me on my mobile if you have any problems and don't hesitate to come spend the night with us. " The centre of this large town (seventy thousand inhabitants) is run down ; some of the older buildings are in a pitiful state. Streetlights are ripped out ; there are tank tracks here and there.

The taxi sets us down at the Jenin North exit, which leads towards the refugee camp. We ask for directions. A young man offers to drive us in his uncle's car and, a kilometre further down the road, drops us off in the middle of the camp. On the whole, the houses demolished in April 2002 have been cleared away. The rain has transformed this wasteland into a bog. Bullet holes scar everything, including the walls of the school. We walk up a street of the camp.

From the hilltops above the camp the refugees can apparently see the villages their families abandoned after 1948. On the ground floor of a bombarded house an old woman in heavy clothing sits near a brazier seeking warmth. Without doors and windows, she is exposed to the winds. Night falls ; it continues to rain ; it's cold ; many residents camp in the ruins.

A smiling young man greets us with a friendly hello. Owing to his English-speaking skills, Jamal has made it his responsibility to welcome visitors to the camp. He is slight and agile, quick in his movements ; he might almost be mistaken for a child. " Welcome. Come in. There is a wedding celebration in the house ! " Jamal introduces his parents, two old people seated on the floor in the kitchen near the fire, away from the festivities. They make room for us on the carpet and offer tea. Nearby women prepare the bride's henna tattoos. Dozens of children stand around, smiling for our camera. I dare not ask the parents about their experiences during the invasion of the camp in April 2002.

This evening my courage fails me. My feet are soaked ; they have been since this morning. If I listened to my self, I would return to Ramallah immediately. But the town is sealed off after six p.m. I realise that I have lost my mobile phone, no doubt in the taxi, Meaning that Ulfa's phone number is also lost. No choice, we will have to spend the night in the town's only hotel and tomorrow try to track down my phone.

Gardens Hotel lies in the heart of the souk ; comfort is Spartan : two beds per room, no heating, reasonable rates (forty shekels, eight euros per night). We are the only guests. The owner kindly seats us near the gas fire, makes tea and helps us dry our coats and socks.

The rain stops ; we are warm again ; I feel my nerve return. We explore the market streets. The pastry shop sells wonderful kenafe (a sweet cheese-filled pastry served warm). Find Ulfa's brother, find Ulfa and maybe, with her help, find the taxi driver and…my mobile phone. The chemist speaks Italian, but she doesn't know the Rashid family. A stroke of luck, I recognise the brother's building. It's seven thirty in the evening ; we knock on the door. The door is opened by a forty year-old man, slender build, calm demeanour. He doesn't understand our explanations ; but so what, hospitality first. We are greeted by a tiny young woman, a native of the refugee camp, she explains. She recently married this man who has seven children from his first marriage. The little ones huddle quietly on the carpets close to their father. It is a large flat and the children show us around ; a room for the four boys, another for the three girls, a room for the parents and a spacious living room where the television is enthroned. On the wall, a picture of the grandfather on horseback, dressed as an officer in the Jordanian army. The large sofa in the living room remains empty ; the family prefers to sit on carpets on the floor near the heater. The children remain silent, observing us inquisitively. Only after we have consumed tea, coffee and cakes does the master of the household call the sister who lives in Jenin. Ulfa ? Yes, she arrived this afternoon. Yes, she had a call from the taxi driver. We should come meet them on the other side of town. In Ulfa's brother's car – an unemployed civil engineer, who recently lost his job – we drive through a totally deserted Jenin at night. Two of his sons accompany us. We come to a stop in front of a remote little house on the heights overlooking the countryside. A large family welcomes us, Ulfa's sister, her husband and six children, and their four cousins who just arrived from Tulkarm. Huddling side-by-side on carpets, they listen attentively to Ulfa's story : how we met ; the journey to Jenin ; the present reunion ; set in the narrative like a jewel, the story of my lost and almost-found telephone. The audience loves the story and begs Ulfa to recount dozens of minor details. In the opinion of the listeners, the most surprising development is how I stumbled across the brother's building again. In my opinion, the most amazing phenomenon is their infinite kindness, their spontaneous bending over backward to help perfect strangers like us.

Last year's sufferings ? What is there to say ? Pictures taken in the refugee camp during and after the siege tell the story. Mutilated corpses. Ruins. People, so horribly wounded, we don't know which way to turn the pictures. White tents set up where the camp's shanty houses once stood. The pictures circulate from hand to hand, even among the children. A six year-old girl, her black hair held together in two thick braids, also looks, stops and stares, then passes on the pictures. Ulfa, ordinarily so talkative, offers only one line of commentary : " It is they who are the terrorists. "

The family plans to visit a young man, almost a miracle survivor, still recovering from his wounds. " Please come along. He will appreciate it. " Seven adults pile into a small Renault car. Ulfa's brother drives ; it is dark ; the rain has finally stopped. The moon rises. We arrive at the wounded survivor's

206

house, a modest villa perched on the heights above Jenin ; in the distance the lights of the Israeli coastal cities are clearly visible. Nineteen year-old Abed has just been released after three months in a Jordanian hospital. Gaunt, very pale. He was standing guard at the security post of the Palestinian Authority when the Israelis attacked last summer. The medical report mentions several bullet wounds to the stomach, the intestines and the pancreas. In the rectangular white-walled room a dozen or so visitors sit together with his brothers and some friends. The new arrivals ask to see the wounds ; Abed lifts his tracksuit to reveal the deep scar on his right side. He speaks very little ; he doesn't have much to add to what has already been told. Once he is fully recovered, he will take up his job again in the police force. " Otherwise, one way or another, I will take up arms to defend my people. " His friends approve in silence. The eldest, I'm told, is in charge of the local Fatah groups. Abed's mother sets a crystal glass full of lemonade in front of each visitor ; candy is also served. The sadness is not feigned ; nor is the solidarity. Out of politeness we spend a few minutes more. Abed's older brother says he abandoned his A-level exams this year to stay with the wounded boy, " I couldn't leave him by himself. "

At the Garden Hotel, Ulfa and her brother try to persuade us to stay with them. " Don't spend the night in this hotel ; please stay with us. You won't be comfortable here. The market noise will wake you up early. Only men sleep here. It's not a suitable place for women like you. " We decline the invitation firmly, but politely, not to upset them.

Friday morning. There is no market today ; the centre of Jenin is empty. During the night we heard the rumble of gunfire far in the distance. We learn that the army entered the refugee camp at four a.m. to make an arrest; two or three people died in the fighting. A curfew has been imposed again. Long wait before a collective taxi for Tulkarm fills up. At the edge of the city a helmeted soldier perched on a tank inspects documents. He sits two metres above the road; a Palestinian stretches his arm to hand him a green document holder with his ID. In Tulkarm, Khaled, Ulfa's husband, hands me my mobile phone that he has already fetched from the taxi driver. " Please don't thank me. Have a good trip ! " Another change of taxi at the Anabta checkpoint. By noon we are back in Ramallah ; the sky is bright and sunny again.

14 January. This morning we learn that a young woman from Gaza blew herself up at the Erez security post. Four dead, ten wounded, mostly military. The suicide attack is claimed by Hamas and the Al Aqsa Martyrs Brigade. New development, the suicide bomber is a twenty year-old mother of two. Until now Hamas has refused to involve women in attacks. Israeli authorities announce a tightening of the lock up in Gaza and a suspension of permits for the thirty thousand workers that still have one. I read the young woman's last declaration in Haaretz : " I will knock on the door of heaven with the skull of a Jew. " I remember Sergeant Blumberg : is his name on the victim list ? No details today. Israeli operations continue in Rafah, more deaths, dozens more buildings demolished.

Visit to Givat Shaül cemetery, Jerusalem West. Purpose of the visit : find my grandmother's tomb. The cemetery has no information desk as such, only a few old men, some bearded, some clean shaven ; they look like they might know. One speaks to me in French. " What was your grandmother's name ? Hmm, she wasn't Sephardic. Not my speciality. Some of us know the Persians, others the Iraqis, others the Ethiopians. " And the Ashkenazim ? " Nobody. – What do you mean nobody ? – Just like I said. Can't you hear ? " There is a phone number on the closed door of a shack ; in case of absence call… A voice answers in Hebrew. I try English, no. Russian ? Da. I'm in luck. The person's father, an old man by the name of Avram, is somewhere in the vicinity ; maybe he can help. I find the old man – shabby old suit, large staved-in hat, unkempt white beard, crumbs scattered all over his clothes – slumped in a corner. He looks absolutely destitute ; I took him for a beggar earlier. Hebrew and Yiddish only ; this will not be easy. He opens the shack and agrees to check through a stack of papers. Family name ? I spell it in English : it doesn't ring a bell. Christian name ? Lea. Daughter of ? Benjamin. There is no lack of Leas daughters of Benjamins in Givat Shaül cemetery. Patience. Sheets of paper fly in every direction. I slip a few shekels into the piggybank with a Star of David on the side ; maybe that will help. Twenty-five minutes later, after a call to a friend of my family living in Israel, I locate my grandmother's tomb. 1895-1993. Almost a century. And what a century ! Bright sunshine and tranquil silence. Not many visitors, a few Russians, garden tools in hand. The cemetery's divisions rise in tiers up the steep slopes that overlook the Jerusalem-Tel-Aviv highway ; cypresses silhouette the horizon. The graves, tightly squeezed together, speak many languages Hebrew, Russian, Greek, English, French. It's as international as Ben Gurion airport. If my grandmother feels anything now, she must feel good to be here, in this land she loved so passionately. Only a small " s " would chagrin her. On the headstone is engraved the following line in French : " tendres souvenirs de ses petits-enfants et arrières-petits-enfants ". The incriminating " s " that clings to " arrière " has been scraped off as far as possible ; but the Satanic serpent's hiss startles all the more now that dirt has filled the shallow cavity. Lea's perfectionism was legendary ; as far as French grammar and vocabulary were concerned she was intractable. How would she take the mistake ? With a sense of humour ? I think so. But she would surely not take my chronicles from Ramallah lightly. Never mind. My visit is just a small expression of tenderness. My grandmother silently regretted our disagreements, but resigned herself to them ; they never dried up her

210

feelings. Faithful to our Jewish tradition, I place a pebble on the head stone. On the " s " of course.

My stay in Palestine is nearly at an end. The film production team has gone back to France. I welcome two more French friends, a poet and a philosopher. Each has his reasons for taking an interest in Palestine. I lodge them at my home in Ramallah ; yes, my home ; even if it is " mine " only a little while longer.

25 January. Abu Dis is hardly recognizable. On my last visit a low wall split the main street in two ; it was easy to hop over it. Today it is a huge wall erected in the middle of town, barely three metres from buildings, all slated for demolition. Shops are closing one after the other. The chemist remarks : " It was a lively place where business was good. Now I can't even sell the premises ; they're worthless. Twenty-five years down the drain. I'll have to start all over again on the other side. "

The wall is just as high as in Tulkarm and Qalqiliya (eight metres), but instead of winding around the town, it cuts it in half. The Palestinian population finds itself torn apart as well ; some are being annexed to Jerusalem suburbs, others cast off to the Barbarians. The immediate impact is that the Wall separates children from their schools, students from their university, the faithful from Al Aqsa mosque, the sick from their dispensary and the workers from their livelihood. And tensions rise a few more degrees.

27 January. Nablus. Hotel Yasmeen. I bump into Benjamin again, a young French journalist I come across from time to time here. My friends wander the alleys of the souk – a marvel of sights, sounds and smells – I prefer to spend the afternoon with

Benjamin. The upcoming prisoner exchange with Hizbollah may create the opportunity to table the case of Said el-Atabeh, the longest held political prisoner in Palestine. At three p.m. we knock on the front door of the Atabeh family house. A strangely designed house ; one enters through a bathroom. Sanah Atabeh, slender, matching brown jacket and trousers that look almost like a man's suit, nicely cut short hair ; she looks the part of an executive. Her English is faultless ; when it does fail, she has some Russian. Profession : administrator of NGOs in the health and welfare sector, now a full-time mother, unemployed. Her aging mother, veiled, is seated in an armchair. She understands no English but approves from time to time with cups of coffee and cakes. There is no window in the living room. Picture portraits of Said el-Atabeh and a tiny dove of peace made of bonded pearls hang on the walls. On a low table, a one metre square miniature model of the Al Aqsa mosque, made in the same technique as the dove of peace.

Sanah Atabeh's story.

" My brother Said was arrested on July 29, 1977. He was twenty-six years old. He was the leader of a small group that he had formed in Nablus. First, his companions were taken ; then, a week later he was arrested. The army didn't demolish the house because only half of it belonged to us. Anyway the soldiers impounded two rooms, cut off water and electricity and walled them up. Every two months they came by to check that we hadn't broken the seals. When Arafat returned in 1994, we were able to recover our two rooms. Since then we enlarged the house on the other side, as you saw when you arrived.

" In 1978 Said was found guilty and sentenced to life in prison. We knew the sentence would be harsh, because three judges presided over the verdict. The group had carried out two attacks, one in Haifa and one in Tel Aviv. Said was found guilty, though he did not place the bombs himself. He was also found guilty for his secret six-month stay in Syria and for his contacts with the PLO. Said was a member of the Democratic Front (DFLP). Later, in 1992, he joined the FIDA, a small party that supports the peace process since the Madrid conference.

" Our family was communist. My father was not very militant, but my uncle was very active in the liberation movement under Jordanian rule. He was sentenced to be hanged, but was pardoned by the king ; he was imprisoned near the Iraqi border in Jiffer where he served a long sentence.

" Said has been in several military prisons. When he was in Ashkelon, we visited him every two weeks, as long as we had a travel permit. We left at three a.m. to be there by seven. Then we had to wait outside the entire day. At first we only had twenty minutes with him. After five years of struggle and hunger strikes, our visits increased to forty minutes. It was very hard ; there was so much noise and so many people, we could hardly hear each other. On one side of the room there were thirty prisoners, behind them a cordon of soldiers ; on the other side, ninety visitors and another cordon of soldiers. Between the two a metal screen with meshes so tight we could barely poke a finger through. If we stood up, the soldiers forced us to sit down again immediately. We weren't allowed to bring anything ; no food, no books, only warm clothes for the winter ; and money, no cash, only cheques. Before each visit, we were stripped naked and searched. Inside our mouth, everywhere. Even our shoes.

" For the past three years we have been denied a travel permit, so we haven't seen him. We send him clothing through the Red Cross and the Palestinian Red Crescent. We talk by phone, in secret, of course.

" Said is the longest held political prisoner in Palestine, the third longest held in the world. Twenty-seven years ; fifty-four Eids we have spent without him ! He has never met my husband or my sister's husband. He has never seen our children ! My father always visited him. He died of a heart attack in 1989, December 14th, two days after visiting him. At the time Said was being held in the Negev. There was a curfew, tear gas. Because of the curfew, my father had to walk home. He was my father and my friend.

" At the same time as Said, another of my brothers was arrested ; later he became a doctor. They were arrested on the wedding day of my sister who lives in the United States now. After secondary school, Said studied to become an electrician, but at the time he was delivering Coca-Cola bottles to shops. I was fifteen years old and still in school. Later I went to the Soviet Union for my higher education and earned a degree in public health. That's where my other brother studied medicine.

" Many prisoners have since been released. The men of Said's group were exchanged in 1985. There have been other well-publicised prisoner exchanges since then. We have waited and waited, and hoped ; but nobody has ever done anything for Said ; not the NGOs ; not the Palestinian Authority ! If he had been a Fatah member, he would have been exchanged. Arafat told us " he's at the top of the list ", but he was

214

never on a list ! I am very angry at the Palestinian Authority. Our second Intifada was also against the Authority.

" Said is much more moderate than me. In prison they call him Abul Hakkam, Father of Wisdom, the conciliator. He condemns all attacks without exception and he continues to support the peace process. He has even learned some Hebrew. He remains an atheist and refuses to fast during Ramadan. In the same cell there are thirty-five prisoners belonging to different organisations ; many are believers ; Said became a close friend of a very pious man who came to see us after his release. They might never have become friends had they met outside prison.

" Following one particular strike they won the right to have a television. Said also listens to the radio ; he reads and he takes thirty minutes of exercise every day with his fellow prisoners. We manage to speak together, though signals are frequently scrambled. He buys phones from corrupt soldiers who wheel and deal ; he pays with code numbers we provide. This costs us about a thousand shekels a month (one hundred eighty five euros). Said calls every other day. For a year now he has been in love with a woman he met over the phone, the daughter of one of his prison friends. She visited us here yesterday.

" My mother is seventy-five years old and diabetic. She thinks about him all the time. During celebrations, she no longer makes the cakes he used to like so much. When she drinks coffee, she thinks of Said who loved coffee. She would like to hold him in her arms on more time. She won't live forever.

" Said published a book. His fellow prisoners have published testimonials in his favour. They even erected a huge portrait of him on Al Manara Square. But nothing happens.

" Sometimes Said and I joke on the phone : 'I'll be home this evening. – OK I'll make some tea.' It has been ten thousand days since he was last home ! "

Wednesday. 28 January. An uneventful trip back from Nablus. Before leaving Ramallah for Paris, scheduled for Saturday, I must pack my bags, pay my rent and say goodbye to my Palestinian friends. Sally calls : " Majid, your neighbour's eldest son, has been arrested. " The news shatters me. Majid is one of the most moderate Palestinians I know. A young family man, he works for the Ministry of Foreign Affairs ; his life is very bourgeois, very quiet. He washes and polishes his car every Friday. He's the one who told me last October : " Your Mr de Villepin is right : the Palestinian Authority has to be tougher on the militant groups ; we must impose order. " Mrs Huzri never leaves the house anymore, except to hang laundry on the terrace we share. Her husband, the professor, who wears very strict suits, is gloomier than ever. Mussa has taken a leave from the bank to look after his family. He knocks on my door with his sister-in-law : " Do you have any email addresses of human rights organisations ? We don't even know where Majid is being held. "

Thursday. 29 January. Another bomb attack on a bus in Jerusalem. Ten dead, at least forty wounded. Severe clamp down on the West Bank. The suicide bomber was from Bethlehem. Military operation in the Aida refugee camp. On-going operation in Rafah ; reports of several dead, various buildings demolished.

Friday. 30 January. Mussa has news about his brother. A lawyer, who regularly makes the rounds of Israeli prisons, came across Majid's name on the register of the OFRA detention centre (ten kilometres outside Ramallah). He is being held in secret ; nevertheless the family is relieved. How was Majid arrested ? " A friend showed up at one a.m. looking for a place to sleep. At three a.m. the Israelis arrived and took them both away. Fortunately, his friend didn't try to defend himself ; otherwise they would have blown up the house. They searched everywhere ; everything in the house is destroyed. – Were his wife and little Luna at home ? – Yes, but nobody touched them ; they're fine. – And the friend, who is he ? – A childhood friend. He leads the Al Aqsa Martyrs Brigade in Ramallah. He'll be sentenced to life in prison. He was probably being tailed when he arrived at my brother's flat. "

My neighbour, Georgette, invites me over for a last cup of tea. " A friend asks for help ; of course we help. This is how we are brought up, to help our neighbour. Christian or Muslim, it doesn't matter ; you'll never see a Palestinian refuse hospitality to a friend being hunted by the Israelis. Nobody can sleep outside every night ! "

All my friends in Ramallah pay me a final goodbye visit. Hands full of small gifts. I had planned a tiny farewell party. I abandon the plan ; there is too much grief in the flat next door.

Saturday. 31 January. Early. Mrs Huda comes by to pick up the keys. While I collect my bags and take a last look around the flat, my landlady consoles my neighbour ; she is taking down her laundry and folding it in a large basket. Her head covered in her usual

brown headscarf ; her body wrapped in her
embroidered long green coat ; Mrs Huzri's features are
still drawn. She has not stopped crying for three days.

AFTERWORD

In December 2005 I went back to Palestine. Twenty-two months had gone by since my last chronicle entry; almost two years of earthshaking events that History may choose to remember: Israeli army assassinations of Sheikh Yassine (the spiritual leader of Hamas) and Dr Rantissi; the death of Yasser Arafat; the election of Mahmoud Abbas to the presidency; the ceasefire agreement concluded in Cairo; the evacuation of Jewish settlements in Gaza; the opening of the Rafah border post; the election of Amir Peretz as head of the Labour Party; the creation of the centrist party Kadima by Ariel Sharon; the success of Hamas in the municipal elections. As I write, other events capture the headlines: Ariel Sharon's disappearance from the public stage; the implosion and debacle of Fatah; the electoral victory of Hamas; the ultimatum of the Western powers; impending Israeli elections.

During this new stay in Palestine I see, hear and learn many things.

Between Ramallah and the Arab suburbs of Jerusalem, the razor barbed wire and yellow barriers have been replaced by concrete almost everywhere. As far as the eye can see, the wall shears through the hills, severs roads, slices through the middle of urban areas. From Kalandia the neighbouring village of A-Ram is no longer visible, only an endless grey wall, tall cylindrical-shaped watchtowers breaking its monotony. Whether you are in Tulkarm, Qalqiliya or Bethlehem, it's the same wall, the same pre-fabricated slabs, assembled according to the same layout. Each slab measures one metre wide by eight metres high. In the upper portion a round opening allows lifting equipment to remove the slab from the lorry, raise it and set it in vertical position, all in one easy movement. The lower portion is a three-metre base, which in cross-section has the shape of a flattened triangle. Each slab is set side by side directly on the roughly cleared ground without foundations. Owing to this mass-production concept and a sizeable budget of two thousand million dollars, two-hundred-twenty kilometres of this wall have been completed in just two and a half years, a third of the planned total. No doubt an innovation with a promising future.

From a Palestinian perspective the wall blocks the horizon both literally and figuratively. It permanently establishes the future final border (otherwise why spend so much money ?) and it blocks the creation of a Palestinian state. Because the wall not only amputates several dozen square kilometres from the West Bank, fragmenting it into three disconnected cantons, it also deprives the future State of its capital, East Jerusalem. Exit the peace process ; the wall is war.

Brandishing once again their rights, the Palestinians are proved right before the International Court of Justice in the Hague and the General Assembly of the United Nations, where it is decided that Israel can build its " security fence " only inside the Green Line. Before Israel's Supreme Court the villagers of Beit Sourik, walled in on all sides, obtain only a small change to the original plan, granted for humanitarian reasons.

Coming from Ramallah to the north or from Bethlehem to the south, if you intend to cross through the wall, you have to use the new " terminals ", which look remarkably like border posts. They are vast hangars covered with sheet metal, entered through a series of turn-styles. Inside one finds the security equipment of a modern prison : remote-controlled doors, electronic gateways, luggage scanners, bomb-proof glass, video surveillance cameras. This new design – " secure, fast, hygienic " according to the Israeli media – allows soldiers to avoid physical contact with the Palestinian mob. Traffic has now diminished considerably, either because there are fewer people with proper travel permits or because these new high-tech terminals inspire even more revulsion than the old checkpoints.

As for the efficiency of the wall in preventing suicide attacks, the issue is controversial.

For several months the residents of the Palestinian village of Bil'in, twenty kilometres west of Ramallah, have been demonstrating peacefully against the construction of the barrier that will cost them half their land and nearly three thousand olive trees. On January 1, 2006 Gush Shalom organised a solidarity rally right in the middle of the expropriated land.

Coming from Bil'in I had to cross a military road lined with barbed wire to gain access to the meeting point (curiously the crossing point was open and unguarded). On the other side, a few olive trees are still standing, though bulldozers have cleared everything else around them. Some sixty Israeli activists and twenty Palestinian villagers are huddled around a huge Hanukah candlestick stuck in the ground. Together they light the last candle of the Jewish festival and Uri Avnery delivers a very ecumenical speech against the occupation. When night falls and the Israeli activists are ready to return to Tel Aviv, they walk back to their two buses, parked fifty metres down the slope on the parking lot of the new settlement Matityahu East. In eight months an eight-storey housing complex has sprouted up ; several flats appear to be occupied already. On the parking lot, two boys with kippahs and locks zigzag on their mountain bikes ; they stop and stare at us dumbstruck. This entire town quarter is set aside for numerous poor Orthodox Jewish families ; they are able to buy their flats thanks to the generosity of North American donors. According to Bimkom, a non-governmental organisation defending planning rights in the territory, property despoliation is an organised system here. The case of Matityahu East involves a Palestinian embezzler, counterfeiting his neighbours' signature to sell land (he was gunned down recently in Ramallah), an Israeli racketeer, a settlers' association and, last but not least, some so-called " civil " administration officials, who money-laundered the entire operation. The result : three thousand flats built on stolen land without a permit and in violation of official planning processes. The army bulldozers and the property developers are obviously in cahoots.

The landscape is changing rapidly too. When I compare the pictures I took in 2003 with those I take today, the changes are eye-stopping. New roads appear, new housing estates. Communicating vessels ? In just four months since the evacuation of Gaza, six thousand new settlers have rallied to the West Bank. The number of Jewish Israelis now living on the other side of the Green Line approaches the half million mark. Most live inside the perimeter of the wall on lands that have been de facto annexed. A further ninety thousand settlers, whose fates are not yet sealed, live scattered throughout the West Bank. Israel plans to remove some one hundred " illegal outposts " but is already showing signs of alarm at the resistance the young radical settlers are likely to put up. And just where will the future border lie ? Along the Jordan River or along the barrier ? No major political party – not Labour, not the Centre, not the Right – proposes a return to the Green Line. For ages Europe has held firm to UN resolutions. But in the past two years, it has moved closer to the position of the American administration, which argues " a return to pre-1967 borders would not be realistic ". " Europe has disappointed us. In practice, confides Dr Rita Giacaman wearily, there is no longer any difference with the United States. "

Trusting in collective punishment, the army pursues its policy of locking down towns and cities after each terrorist attack. During the lull, in 2005 traffic circulation between West Bank urban areas improved slightly. I managed to visit Jenin, Hebron and even Nablus without too much difficulty. But the flow is relative ; since last spring access to the Jordan Valley and Jericho is practically cut off. Road traffic can be interrupted without notice. Last Saturday, the day I arrived, Kalandia was closed. Two days before, Sergeant Nir Kahana, twenty, on guard at the Kalandia checkpoint, was knifed to death by Yussef Abu-Adi, twenty-nine, acting alone ; he was immediately apprehended. The media quickly reported that the Palestinian aggressor was a mental patient, who had recently been released from a psychiatric hospital. The terminal reopened on Tuesday to a slow trickle. Pedestrians had to wait at least two hours, vehicles up to five. As for Gaza, though it is now evacuated, it has not been liberated. Israelis still control directly all access points except for Rafah. Each closure results in the loss of hundreds of workdays and tons of perishable goods. Each lock down makes the chaos a little worse.

After the tragedy of 2002 the economy gradually improved. In certain cities, such as Ramallah, Hebron and Jenin, growth is visible with the naked eye. The number of building sites is on the rise ; shopping centres are opening ; long queues of delivery vehicles now block access to markets. A Palestinian stock market recently opened in Nablus ; like elsewhere, even under the green flags of Hamas, it is now possible to dabble in financial speculation. The ruins of 2002 have almost disappeared. Even the Muqataa compound looks better with its new administrative buildings and a real gate guarded by soldiers in uniform. International aid has helped the residents of the Jenin camp to build small modern houses on the former ruins. Not everybody enjoys the benefits of progress : forty-three per cent live below the poverty line, fifteen per cent in extreme poverty. Rural people suffer most, especially those who have lost land. " We see more and more malnourished children with loss of hair ; they are the living dead ", Rita Giacaman informs me ; she is in charge of public health operations in the northern villages. " Youths hang around doing nothing. No future, no work, no money to study, no prospect of marriage. Such frustration. It's a time bomb ! " In Bethlehem, formerly a prosperous locality, foreign pilgrims have virtually disappeared, hotels are empty. At midnight mass, among the few visitors from Israel, one notices the one hundred or so Filipino household employees in particular. Across from the new terminal, which regulates access to the walled community, the parking lot is empty ; the huge propaganda billboard that the Israeli Ministry of Tourism has affixed to the concrete wall to the right of the watch tower bears a message that no longer draws a smile : Peace be with you.

The death, in November 2004, of Abu Amar, as he was widely known in Palestine, caused much shock – there was talk of poisoning, a Mossad crime, dread of a succession war. Then, very rapidly, the emotional pitch fell. " The day after the funeral, a friend told me, everybody went about their business as usual, as if nothing had happened. " Pictures of the former president still hang here and there, papered to the lions in Al-Manara Square, stuck on the walls of Nablus and Ramallah, sellotaped to every surface in schools, health dispensaries and shops. They are not official portraits, rather pictures taken from magazines ; posters printed in a hurry and hung up wherever it strikes one's fancy. One of the best is a huge pixellated portrait made of a thousand small pictures : men, women and children from Palestine. Arafat's picture is common property. On Fatah posters he stands facing Mahmud Abbas, his finger raised in a lecturing gesture. On Hamas reproductions he is seated next to Sheikh Yassine ; the faces of the two deceased leaders touch as if they were raising their glasses in a toast to each other.

Affection for the father of the nation does not preclude a " right of assessment ". Above all the Oslo Accords : so poorly negotiated, one might think Arafat had only one concern, his own return to Palestine. Personal power : he took every decision himself, even on issues of the least importance, sapping the authority of his Ministers. Archaism : he failed to consult the population on important decisions, relied on clan heads, manoeuvred between the great families. Secret finances : for every service rendered to the cause, he expressed thanks with a few bank notes extracted from a mysterious suitcase that never left his side. George Khleifi, the television producer, recalls the broadcasting in Bethlehem of the first Christmas mass attended by Arafat. Pleased with the technical results, the president himself gave each technician two hundred dollars in cash. Errors of judgement : the list would be too long to establish.

The most consensual topic is corruption. For once Israelis and Palestinians agree on this. Since 1997 huge scandals have tarnished several individuals close to the Authority. Without results : no judicial enquiry, no trial, no sanctions. Worse, suspects have enjoyed the protection of accomplices, who helped them escape with their spoils. Granted, corruption may be no worse than in other Arab regimes (far from it indeed), but after five years of Intifada, Palestinians

226

can no longer put up with it. All the more since the Authority owes its existence to a popular uprising. The population believes it has the right to demand an accounting. On a day-to-day basis, it is the clientelism above all else that undermines trust. The bulk of the Palestinian Authority's budget is used to pay the salaries of one hundred-thirty-five thousand civil servants, half of them assigned to security forces. Knowing Fatah, it isn't hard to imagine who gets the jobs. The one hundred-thirty-five thousand salaries keep one quarter of the population alive. This is not a small matter.

The police are one of the few sectors that still hire young people. They can be seen strolling around Al-Manara Square in their multi-coloured uniforms, too large for their frames, looking like adolescents having a good time together. They are supposed to turn up stolen cars (there are plenty) and arrest drivers without permits (virtually all the young ones). But enthusiasm does not stretch to the arrest of friends fooling around in stolen cars. And when the Israeli tanks arrive in force to arrest a suspect and terrorise the population, the young recruits vanish into thin air. Around Kalandia a few trainee police would be helpful to direct traffic, but according to the Oslo Accords the zone is exclusively under Israeli security control. So an older civilian, not wearing a uniform, does the job and receives a few tips from drivers. Recently a senior police officer from France arrived to set up police training programmes in Ramallah ; he had worked in a similar capacity in Kosovo. " Nobody knows the code of penal procedures ", he tells me. " Earning a hundred fifty euros per month, you can't expect them to achieve miracles. " His mission in

Palestine is scheduled to last three years. People say to him Mabrouk ! (" Good luck "), somewhat soberly.

Thanks to a quota system adopted in 2004 women have joined politics in number. Over a thousand now sit on municipal councils ; one of them, Janet Mikhail, recently captured the Ramallah city hall. A relaxed Christian woman, elected at the head of the " Ramallah for All " list. Because her list of independent democrats won the same number of seats as Fatah (six), Hamas (three seats) provided the additional votes that made her the first Palestinian woman to become mayor. Janet Mikhail granted me an interview a few days before her election. Without campaign headquarters or an official campaign office, she came to see me at the French cultural centre. She had been head teacher of the girls' school in Ramallah for twenty years ; it was in this role that she won the trust of her fellow citizens. Her programme does not promise miracles, simply better, more rigorous administration ; she vows to be closer to the people of all political stripes and faiths. Officially she has no binding agreement with Hamas, but she is weighing the option of offering it the portfolio for social affairs. " We will have no difficulty working together. The general interest must prevail. "

Women – foremost mothers and widows of shahid (" martyrs ") – are very active in Hamas and in the charitable organisations it controls. They represent an overwhelming majority of its electorate. This fact, which greatly surprises foreign observers, goes to show that Hamas enjoys a reputation for order, honesty and discipline in Palestine. Moreover the national Islamist movement does not hold a threatening discourse against the recognised rights of women. " My wife drives a car, my daughters attend university ", the lawyer Rabi H. Rabi is quick to tell me.

This recently elected Hamas counsellor does not live clandestinely, does not wear a beard or djellaba. His office is located on the high street, above Rukab, the best ice cream shop in Ramallah. A prominent citizen in his fifties, wearing a light coloured suit and tie, small moustache, he speaks like a family man respectful of traditions and of the diversity that is typical of his city. " Ramallah is neither Hebron, nor Gaza. We have no intention of imposing anything. Islam commands us to be honest, hard working, charitable towards the needy ; that is what people expect from us, here and everywhere in Palestine. "

I have not come across any frightened secular women. The architect Souad Amiry, who told me two years earlier " I prefer Sharon to Hamas ", laughs heartily. " Did I really say that ? What idiocy ! " Another secular woman tells me, " Before Hamas gets involved in issues that divide our society, it will have other more urgent matters to attend to. "

The anarchy that rages in Gaza has not won the West Bank. No one has taken to kidnapping foreigners or occupying Ministries. But the dissensions within Fatah itself do leave a bad impression here in December 2005. In the voting precincts where the party organises its primary elections, political debate is often settled with a burst of Kalashnikov fire (in the air). Two Fatah lists, both led by Marwan Bargouti, were registered, then withdrawn before being merged. " They do not reflect two opposing party lines, rather two sets of personal ambition ", says Anouar Abu Eisheh, law professor and Fatah activist in Hebron.

" In the primary elections we tick the names of people we know. Most people tick the names of the heads of the security forces because they are best known. "

I have not been able to obtain the necessary permits to travel to Gaza. " Too dangerous " objects the French consul. " Unnecessary " says the civil servant in the Israeli Ministry of Information. I must be content to collect testimonies and read newspaper accounts. All the same, aren't the medias confusing Gaza and Baghdad ?

The existence of armed factions is nothing new in Palestinian life. But, until recently anyway, the understanding was that their violence was turned solely against Israel. That weapons are used to dictate a balance of power within Palestine itself is a novelty that the majority adamantly rejects. The culprit is a withering of power : " As long as Arafat was in power, the armed factions did not dare to strike at the Authority. " Having said that, in Palestinian eyes the real cause of chaos are the Israelis, their bombardments, armed incursions, demolitions of houses and roads, destruction of olive groves, expropriations, lock downs, economic stranglehold and asphyxiation. What is most astounding is that in the middle of all the chaos so many people manage to work, study, care for their children and simply smile.

" The impression I get is that my students are more confident in the future ; they seem less tempted by suicide attacks than two years ago ", confides George Khleifi who finishes our interview in his office at the university on a positive note. " This is not a repudiation of the resistance or the armed struggle ; it's simply that Israeli reprisals are too much to bear, people have reached their breaking point ", says the philosopher May Jayyusi. In their statistics Israelis do not differentiate between Palestinian attacks that target civilians and those targeting the military. Neither do they discern offensive operations (attacks on a checkpoint or a car, setting an explosive device) from defensive operations (resisting arrest). They label everything " terrorist attack ". In perfect symmetry, as far as Palestinians are concerned, all armed action is " resistance ", a necessary response to the constant aggression they endure. In Nablus, where the French cultural centre has invited me to speak, a student asks : " What do you think about army incursions that kill women and children and about suicide operations ? " The same morning Israeli armoured vehicles entered the city centre, killing a militant and wounding thirty young shebabs, who had been showering them with stones. In my answer I tried to clarify the concepts of resistance and revenge, but I fear my reply was not convincing. It was no time for philosophy.

Palestinians are summoned to give up violence. But violence invades their lives, their history, their everyday being. When my friend May crosses through the new Kalandia terminal she reacts differently than I do, because everything in the experimental setup is an act of violence against her : the stupid signs that invite visitors to keep the place tidy ; the steel turnstiles that open and close, as if for laboratory rats ; the bawling voices that bark orders through loudspeakers in barracks-Arabic ; the security windows, behind which arrogant young female soldiers strut about in bullet-proof vests ; the slot in the wall forty centimetres from the floor that she must almost get on her knees to slide her identity card through ; the residence permit that she risks losing at almost anytime ; the propaganda board that cynically proclaims in three languages (Arabic, Hebrew, English) The hope of us all. And, above all else, the concrete wall that stretches as far as the eye can see, lacerating the countryside around Jerusalem, blocking access to the city where she found love, raised her children, developed her curiosity, knowledge and friendship ; the city where she believed she was at home. Who sees this violence ? Who will make it stop ?

Epilogue. I paid a visit to some of the people who unawares became characters in my chronicles in 2003-2004. Good news. Majid, Mrs Huzri's son, was quickly released from prison and his family breathes comfortably again. Sari Hanafi left to teach sociology at the American University of Beirut. Faroun, Malika's nephew, got married and recently opened a restaurant-bar that serves a wide range of wines and alcoholic drinks. His patriotic and secular convictions have not softened in the least. Liza Tamari's two little girls have grown and the flat itself seems bigger. " Now that the Surda checkpoint has been lifted, we leave our curtains open and enjoy the view. " Liza has no fear of the future. " Anyway it can't get worse. " In the Jenin refugee camp, Djamal has taken a job on the police force. Because he hates guns (" too many friends died "), he makes sandwiches for the police station. He continues to work as a volunteer interpreter-guide just for fun.

Now for some less cheerful news. Bachar, the rocker computer geek, is leaving for the United States. " Because I haven't succeeded in putting my documents in order, I have to return to Jordan every month to renew my tourist visa. It's ruining me. As for work, no Palestinian business can afford to hire some one with my expertise. There's a management position waiting for me in Florida. After that I hope to create a company with some friends in San Francisco. And, frankly, the idea of living under the lead screed of Islamism makes my blood run cold. " At the Elias home – they are long-standing Fatah activists – spirits are low. " We have lived our entire lives for this cause and we are reaching a dead-end ", confides Sally. " The next generation has to start on a more pragmatic basis, maybe founding a new party. After all, Sharon did it, why not us ? " Georgette Khoury welcomed me gravely as well. Her son Shadi almost died on May 31, 2004 when a bullet stopped only a centimetre from his heart. " The Israelis were on Al-Manara Square in pursuit of a car, shooting in all directions. As a precaution, Shadi decided to close the jewellery shop where he works as an employee. A stray bullet went through a four millimetre-thick reinforced door ! He needed sixteen blood transfusions. Thankfully young people from all over came to give blood at the hospital, which was full of wounded that day. Shadi's wife was at the beginning of her pregnancy and deeply shocked. Happily, everything ended for the best. Shadi went back to work at the end of August and Victor (Nasser in Arabic) was born in November. " Little Victor listens quietly to the story on his grandmother's lap.

In Nablus the El-Atabeh family is still waiting for Said's return. He is starting his twenty-ninth year in prison.

West Bank

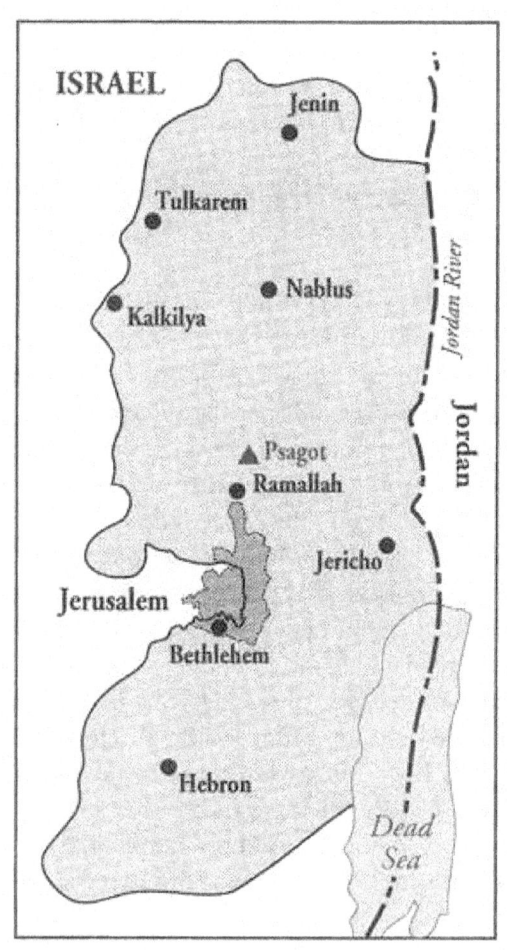

Israel and Palestine

AUTHOR'S NOTE

The quotation on page 5 can be found in Arendt, Hannah. The Jewish Writings, edited by Jerome Kohn and Ron H. Feldman, New York : Schocken Books, 2007.

Some names have been changed for reasons of privacy.

ACKNOWLEDGEMENTS

In Palestine, Sabri Giroud, author of the guide Palestine et Palestiniens, published by Groupe de tourisme alternatif ; Sari Hanafi, former Director of the Palestinian refugee research centre ; May Jayyusi, Executive Director of Muwatin, the Palestinian Institute for the Study of Democracy ; Anne Sibiril, French Cultural Centre in Ramallah ; Salwa Mustapha, Lamis Abu Nahleh, Georgette Khoury.

In Israel, the filmmaker Avi Mograbi, his wife Tammi, his sons Shaül and Michal, for their moral and logistical support. Thanks also to the filmmaker Simone Bitton.

A collective thanks to the personnel of the French Consulate in Jerusalem and to the many Israeli associations, whose websites are rich in statistical data ; in particular Btselem (www.btselem.org), Gush Shalom (www.gush-shalom.org/english) and Ta'ayush (www.taayush.org).

In Paris, thanks to Antoinette Weil for her careful reading of the text, Jaques Burko of Diasporiques, Madeleine Rebérioux (deceased 2005), Nicole Savy, Gilles Manceron of the Ligue des droits de l'homme, Stéphanie David of International Federation of Human Rights.

Thanks to Alain Sebbah, Françoise Bouillot and the many friends and correspondents, who provided me with encouragement through their regular emails.

www.ingramcontent.com/pod-product-compliance
Lightning Source LLC
Chambersburg PA
CBHW060617290526
45793CB00001B/53